O
North Argyll
40 favourite walks

The author and publisher have made every effort to ensure that the information in this publication is accurate, and accept no responsibility whatsoever for any loss, injury or inconvenience experienced by any person or persons whilst using this book.

published by
pocket mountains ltd
The Old Church, Annanside, Moffat, DG10 9HB
pocketmountains.com

ISBN: 978-1-9070254-9-5

A catalogue record for this book is available from the British Library

Contains Ordnance Survey data © Crown copyright and database right 2016, supported by out of copyright mapping from 1945-1961

Printed in Poland

Introduction

Argyll and Bute is the second largest region in Scotland, covering over 7000 square km, yet fewer than 90,000 people live here, almost half of them in areas classified as 'remote rural'.

This guidebook covers a large swathe of Mid and North Argyll, sweeping inland from the fractured western seaboard between Crinan and Appin to Arrochar and Bridge of Orchy on the region's eastern periphery. Between these four points lies a landscape awash with sea lochs, with Inveraray roughly at the geographical centre.

There are no large urban areas here and Oban is the largest settlement. Although the road network and public transport infrastructure are good, many routes feel off the beaten track. This is not only down to the low scattered population but also to the indented coast and its many islands, the sea lochs encroaching deep inland, the elongated freshwater lochs and the mountainous interior – making road travel much more convoluted than direct 'as-the-crow-flies' distances would suggest.

As well as its renowned west coast and its sequence of accessible islands, and many great lochs, tumbling rivers and iconic mountains, this region also boasts ancient, wildlife-rich woodlands and several fine gardens. Add to this the Crinan Canal, often described as 'the most beautiful shortcut in Scotland', and some of the most important historical sites in the country and you have all the makings of a fascinating walking destination.

History

Argyll means 'Coastland of the Gaels', referring to the early Gaelic-speaking Scots, who populated much of Scotland's western seaboard. There is plenty to learn when walking in Mid and North Argyll as a good deal of Scotland's early history rests here, particularly in Kilmartin Glen, where more than 400 prehistoric and historic sites sit within a 10km radius.

The low, rocky hill of Dunadd ('Fort of Add' – the River Add flows around its base), a few miles north of Lochgilphead, rises from Kilmartin Glen and was at the centre of the ancient Kingdom of Dál Riata, the name given to the kingdoms of Scotland and Ireland.

It was where Irish settlers, known as the Scotti, arrived in the 6th century AD, and these people eventually gave their name to Scotland. Some 300 years later, the Gaels of Dál Riata joined the Picts of eastern Scotland to establish the kingdom of Alba, after which the control and influence of Dunadd rapidly waned.

Even before the Scotti arrived, humans had begun to leave their mark on the Argyll landscape. Kilmartin Glen contains several burial cairns and standing stones constructed around 4000 to 5000 years ago, while the rock carvings at nearby Achnabreac are believed to date from the same time. Castle Dounie, near Crinan, and Dun na Cuaiche, above Inveraray, hold the remains of Iron Age forts.

Argyll's history over the last few

3

centuries has been a turbulent one, with many battles fought over the loch-bound Castle Stalker, near Appin, Dunstaffnage Castle, a little north of Oban, and Gylen Castle, perched on a rocky outcrop on the island of Kerrera.

These strongholds held strategic positions along the coast and bore witness to civil warfare between rival clans (particularly the Stewarts, Campbells and MacDougalls) and seaboard battles with Viking raiders.

More recently, the landscape has been utilised for agriculture, fuel and timber. The islands of Easdale and Luing were central to the slate industry that for more than 200 years roofed a huge number of Scotland's buildings, while Lismore, a little off the coast from Port Appin, had a thriving limestone industry. These provided employment for thousands of people over the course of the 18th and 19th centuries, as did the Bonawe Iron Furnace during its 123 years of production.

It is only in the last 70 years that the road network and public transport infrastructure have opened up Mid and North Argyll. Prior to this, ferries were a standard mode of transport, linking many isolated rural communities both on the islands and along the indented sea lochs.

Today it is the outdoors industry, including walking, cycling, sailing and wildlife-watching, that is central to a local economy which is still predominantly rural. Lochgilphead remains the region's main administrative centre and – along with towns and villages such as Appin, Arrochar, Benderloch, Inveraray and Oban – provides an ideal base for exploring.

The natural environment

The landscape of Argyll has many facets; great muscular mountains such as Ben Cruachan, low-lying agricultural plains along its centre and little islands cast adrift from the mainland yet only requiring a short ferry journey into a more peaceful, timeless backdrop. The elongated sea lochs of Etive, Fyne and Linnhe claw deep into the coastline while their freshwater cousins, including Loch Awe and Loch Avich, punctuate huge swathes of forest and woodland.

The rocks that form the basis of Argyll date back more than 600 million years to the Dalradian Period, while the obvious arrangement of the land on a southwest to northeast plane is down to an earth movement that occurred 470 million years ago – look at a map of Argyll and you can see the parallel lochs, valleys and ridges trending northeast from the coast.

Mid and North Argyll is also home to some of the best remnants of the renowned oakwoods that once cloaked much of Europe's Atlantic seaboard. Examples can be found at Crinan, Dalavich and Glen Nant, dating back some 7000 years when oak, along with birch, elm and hazel, began to colonise this rough, rocky setting, aided by a warm, moist climate.

Around 6000 years ago, Mid and North Argyll was a dense, temperate rainforest with many now extinct animals, including bears and wolves, hunted by humans. Over time, the forest was cleared ever more extensively, and the human impact on the land has continued apace – from cereal cultivation, introduced some 800 years ago, right up to the present day with the hydroelectric schemes at Loch Glashan and within Ben Cruachan.

This is, nevertheless, a landscape still populated by much wildlife; from the humble redstart and pied flycatcher in summer woodlands through to guillemots and terns on the coast and, of course, the kings of the skies, golden and white-tailed sea eagles.

How to use this guide

Almost all of the walks in this guide can be completed within half a day, leaving plenty of time to explore the natural attractions and historic sites you encounter along the way. Many of the walks are accessible by bus or train while several are reached by a short ferry journey. Basic public transport information is included in this guide, but details/times can change so please check before you set out (travelinescotland.com).

The majority of the routes are low-level and take advantage of Argyll's excellent network of paths. It is not advisable to stray from the routes onto farmland or near exposed cliffs and, where livestock is present, dogs must be kept on leads.

A few of the routes cross steep hill or mountain terrain where good mapreading and navigation skills are necessary in poor weather. Winter walking brings distinct challenges, particularly the limited daylight hours, whilst strong winds along the coast and over higher ground can occur throughout the year.

Preparation for a walk should begin before you set out, and your choice of route should reflect your fitness, the conditions underfoot and the regional weather forecasts (mwis.org.uk).

Even in summer, warm, waterproof clothing is advisable and footwear that is comfortable and supportive with good grips is a must.

None of the hillwalks or longer routes in this guide should be attempted without the relevant OS Map or equivalent at 1:50,000 (or 1:25,000) and a compass – and you should know how to navigate using a map and compass.

Under the Land Reform (Scotland) Act of 2003, there is a right of public access to the countryside of Scotland for recreational purposes. This right depends on whether it is exercised responsibly, while landowners have an obligation not to unreasonably prevent or deter those seeking access. The responsibilities of the public and land managers are set out in the Scottish Outdoor Access Code (outdooraccess-scotland.com).

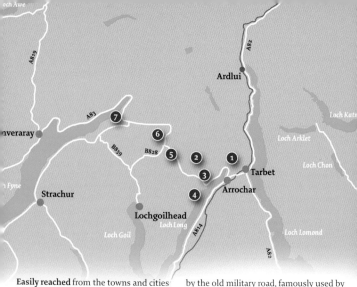

Easily reached from the towns and cities of Scotland's Central Belt, the eastern edge of Mid and North Argyll is dominated by the Arrochar Alps, a range of mountains that rise above Loch Long and have been popular with walkers for decades. Chief among them is The Cobbler, one of Scotland's most iconic peaks, which played an integral role in the Scottish outdoor movement of the 1930s and is still a magnet for hillwalkers today – many of whom try to 'thread the needle' to gain its true summit.

Extending from Loch Long is Glen Loin where a long but pleasant route weaves through woodland with great views and plenty of wildlife to look out for. Almost as well known as the Arrochar Alps is the dramatic Rest and be Thankful, which climbs steeply through Glen Croe. The A83 which runs along here was preceded by the old military road, famously used by travellers that included Samuel Johnson, Thomas Pennant and Dorothy and William Wordsworth. Today, it still makes for a scenic and entertaining walk.

Glen Croe also lies within the Argyll Forest Park, Britain's oldest forest park. The woodland at Ardgartan and the lofty Cat Craig Loop are two walks that take advantage of its paths and tracks.

Soaring high above the Rest and be Thankful are the sharp jagged slopes of Beinn an Lochain, a peak that matches The Cobbler for ruggedness, with an airy ridge and some light scrambling to reach it.

After the Rest gains its 244m high point, it drops down to Loch Fyne and Cairndow. Here, Ardkinglas Woodland Gardens are home to a number of exotic plants and trees, including the Grand Fir, one of Britain's tallest trees.

On the summit of The Cobbler ▸

Arrochar to Loch Fyne

Glen Loin

Distance 16km **Time** 4 hours
Terrain glen and forest paths and tracks
Map OS Explorer 364 **Access** buses from
Glasgow and Oban to Arrochar, 1km from
the start

Set beneath the steep, rocky slopes of
the Arrochar Alps with extensive views
across the Loch Lomond and the Trossachs
National Park, a half-day walk loops round
Glen Loin on good paths and tracks.

From the large car park (charge) at
Succoth, at the western edge of Arrochar,
take care crossing the busy A83, then bear
left to reach the start of a track into the
Argyll Forest Park, zigzagging steeply up
the hillside. A lot of trees have been
cleared here by the Forestry Commission
in recent years, opening up views across
Loch Long to Arrochar.

The meandering climb takes you up to

a T-junction near a radio mast. Turn right to
head northeast along this forest track, high
above Arrochar. At a fork, keep left onto
another track for a descent through
woodland; a stiff ascent then begins,
crossing a footbridge over a waterfall on
the Allt Sugach.

Soon after, the gradient eases and from
here it is a level and very peaceful section
with views of the Arrochar Alps and Ben
Lomond and a carpet of wildflowers all
around in spring and summer. For
hundreds of years the glen was home to
Clan MacFarlane, who were notorious for
their lawless and wild activities. With cattle
reiving at its height during the 16th and
17th centuries there was much bloodshed
between the MacFarlanes and rival clans.

After around 3km, the track turns
northwest and then west above the Allt
Coiregrogain. Loch Sloy dam then comes

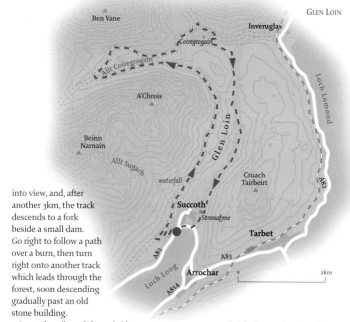

into view, and, after another 3km, the track descends to a fork beside a small dam. Go right to follow a path over a burn, then turn right onto another track which leads through the forest, soon descending gradually past an old stone building.

Beyond a stile and then a bridge, carry on along the track as it sweeps right out of the forest and heads east, with magnificent views of the Loch Lomond hills. Eventually, it curves left and continues under the high, rugged slopes of Ben Vane. After crossing two bridges, the track culminates at a single-track road.

Go right here to follow the road to a track on the right, now taking this towards the remote farm of Coiregrogain. After crossing a bridge, turn left before the farm and go through a gate to reach a path which rises steadily into woodland. In a while, this opens out and a stony path now undulates south over open ground – keep

your eyes peeled for buzzard and roe deer.

Carry on along Glen Loin, eventually passing through a gate. Here the path broadens and crosses a footbridge. Beyond another gate, continue through mixed woodland and then, when the path splits, keep left. Walk past a farmhouse to a fork at Stronafyne.

Bear right and walk down a path that bends sharply right to meet a single-track access road. Turn left to follow this to the A83 at Arrochar, with Loch Long extending south. Carefully cross the road, turn right over a bridge and then go left down steps. Turn right and follow a boardwalk back to the car park.

The Cobbler

**Distance 10.5km Time 5 hours
Terrain hill paths; some steep and
exposed sections Map OS Explorer 364
Access buses from Glasgow and Oban
to Arrochar**

**Apart from Buachaille Etive Mor, there
are few more distinctive peaks in Scotland
than The Cobbler (or Ben Arthur to give it
its proper name), its triptych of peaks
said to resemble a cobbler and his wife
leaning over his last. Thousands of
walkers nearly reach the summit every
year, but only a few dare to thread the
exposed eye of the needle to gain The
Cobbler's true 884m top. Whatever point
you reach, this is one of the finest
hillwalks in the country.**

This route approaches The Cobbler by its
quieter, predominantly pathless southeast
ridge (good navigation skills required in
poor weather), returning by the busier
'tourist' path.

From the large car park (charge) at
Succoth, at the western edge of Arrochar,
take care crossing the busy A83, then
bear left to reach the start of a track into the
Argyll Forest Park, zigzagging steeply up
the hillside.

The meandering climb takes you to a
T-junction near a radio mast. Turn left
here, then right onto a path that weaves its
way northwest up the hillside. In a while, it
runs to the right of the Allt a' Bhalachain
before coming to a small weir, with views
of The Cobbler's magnificent outline.

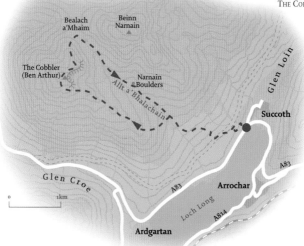

Here, you cross the burn onto grassy slopes and climb evenly in a westerly direction onto the southeast ridge. The ground is reasonably firm and makes for pleasant walking as it rises steadily over a series of rocky undulations towards The Cobbler's obvious South Peak – you may be lucky enough to see red deer roaming the ridge and there are views back to the east to Ben Lomond.

Keep left under the South Peak and then bear right to climb towards the summit, with the rocky pillar of the Centre Peak providing a striking focal point. Its base is the highest point many will reach and it is easy to bypass the true summit, which requires a short but very exposed climb through a hole in the rock – the infamous Eye of the Needle.

Either way, the panorama is spectacular, taking in several of the Arrochar Alps and the Luss Hills, while Loch Long draws the eye to the Firth of Clyde and beyond to Arran. It is also worth exploring the North Peak and its view of the Centre Peak.

Drop north down the main tourist path to the Bealach a' Mhaim, enclosed by the steep sides of Beinn Ime and Beinn Narnain. Now descend southeast along the well-trodden path, passing Lochan a' Chlaidheimh and, further on, ignoring the path that drops down from the main summit ridge on your right.

Continue down to the massive Narnain Boulders, which have provided shelter for several generations of walkers and climbers, particularly during the 1930s when climbing culture first took root in Scotland.

It is now a simple descent, crossing a few burns, back to the outward route beside the weir. Retrace your steps to the car park.

Ardgartan by the Croe Water

Distance 2.25km **Time** 1 hour
Terrain forest and riverside paths and
tracks, minor road **Map** OS Explorer 364
Access buses from Glasgow and Oban
to Ardgartan

The clear, fast-flowing waters of the Croe
are the focal point of this simple and
picturesque walk that meanders through
Ardgartan Forest, part of the Argyll Forest
Park, on the northwest edge of Loch Long.
Ardgartan translates from Gaelic as the
'High Garden' and there are many
interesting plants and flowers to be seen
throughout the year, while in autumn it is
worth coming here to see the blazing
colours of the oak and beech woodland.

The route begins from the car park at
Ardgartan Visitor Centre on the south side
of the A83, 4.5km west of Arrochar (the
visitor centre has limited opening hours).

Walk downhill from the upper car park
and cross a bridge over the Croe Water.
Turn left (signposted for Ardgartan
Peninsula Circuit and hotel) and follow a
minor road southeast, keeping an eye out
for traffic, above the wooded banks of the
river; the steep slopes of Cruach Fhiarach
rise up to the right.

In a while, the road splits. Go left and
follow the Ardgartan Hotel access road
past a distinctive cottage and a lovely old
stone bridge that spans the river.

Carry on along a straight section of road
beneath a canopy of mixed woodland,
with the Croe Water winding its way
towards Loch Long. The river begins its
journey 7.5km to the northwest near the
top of the Rest and be Thankful, in turn
fed by a number of tributary burns
descending from the slopes of The
Cobbler and Ben Donich.

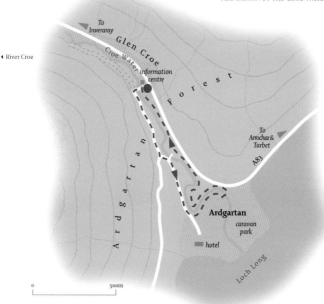

◀ River Croe

To Inveraray

Glen Croe

Croe Water

information centre

F o r e s t

To Arrochar & Tarbet

A83

A r d g a r t a n

Ardgartan

caravan park

hotel

Loch Long

0   500m

On approach to the hotel, the road passes the remains of a cottage and then sweeps left. At the road end, bear left onto a path that then shadows the Croe Water to reach a footbridge. Take this across the river and go left, climb steps and walk towards the A83 and a campsite access road. Just before both, turn left and immediately left again to take a path along the east bank of the river beneath the A83.

After a few metres, keep left at a fork to follow the river, keeping an eye out along its banks for kingfisher and dipper scouring the clear waters for their next meal. There is also a good view of The Brack's craggy profile.

The path proceeds easily along the riverside past several little waterfalls. At a junction, bear left and continue between the river and the A83 with The Cobbler's southern aspect looming ahead. Keep right at the next fork – left leads to the old bridge you passed earlier.

When the trail returns to the riverbank, keep right onto another path and follow this beautiful final section back to the car park.

13

Cat Craig Loop

Distance 9.5km Time 2 hours
Terrain forest paths, tracks, minor road
Map OS Explorer 364 Access buses from
Glasgow and Oban to Ardgartan

A selection of paths and tracks climb
through the Argyll Forest Park, following
the Cat Craig Loop, a great route that
began life as a cycle trail but is now
utilised by walkers. On the way, look out
for wildlife and soak up the views to the
Arrochar Alps and Loch Long.

The route starts from the car park at
Ardgartan Visitor Centre on the south side
of the A83, 4.5km west of Arrochar (the
visitor centre has limited opening hours).
With The Cobbler's craggy summit
towering above you, walk downhill from
the upper car park, cross a bridge over the
Croe Water and turn right onto a wide
forestry track. After passing the lower car

park, this climbs northwest into the
Argyll Forest Park, which was established
in 1935, making it the oldest of Britain's
forest parks.

The woodland above Ardgartan is
predominantly Sitka and Norway spruce
and is home to red squirrel, roe deer and a
host of birdlife. A gradual incline takes
you above the Croe Water along an
enjoyable forest ride. Stick to the main
track, which soon veers left away from the
river and continues to rise steadily, with
views of The Brack's rocky slopes and
Beinn an Lochain's jaggy ridge.

Eventually this brings you to a
junction, where you turn left onto the
waymarked Cat Craig Loop. The trail
undulates easily eastwards, leading to a
viewpoint over The Cobbler's western
slopes as they plunge into Glen Croe. The
conveniently situated picnic table makes

◀ View of The
Cobbler from the
Cat Craig Loop

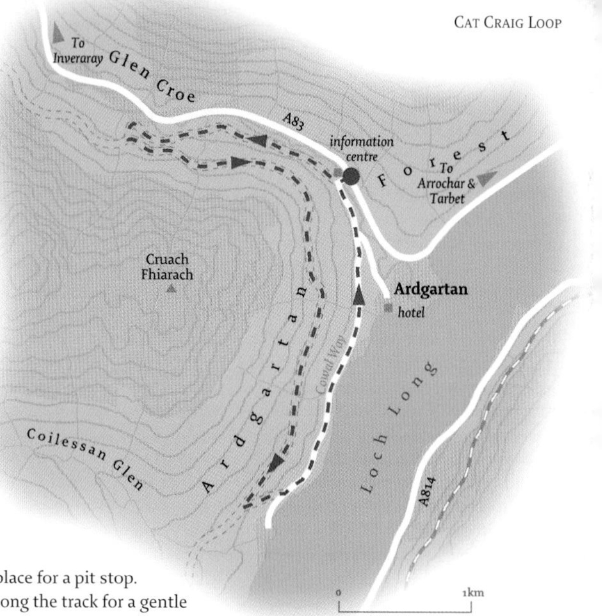

(Map showing Cat Craig Loop area with labels: To Inveraray, Glen Croe, A83, information centre, Forest, To Arrochar & Tarbet, Cruach Fhiarach, Ardgartan, hotel, Cowal Way, Ardgartan, Loch Long, A814, Coilessan Glen)

0   1km

this a good place for a pit stop.

Carry on along the track for a gentle descent back below the treeline and through a tranquil pocket of the forest park with some of the best opportunities for spotting wildlife. Soon comes a prolonged but gradual ascent, the track eventually narrowing to a path. This then zigzags uphill, crossing a footbridge over a burn, with more views – this time along the waters of Loch Long to the village of Arrochar, nestling between Cruach Tairbeirt and Ben Reoch. Loch Long means 'Loch of the Ships', which may refer to the Viking boats that once berthed here before being carried across the narrow isthmus to Loch Lomond.

Take the path that peels left from the main track and drops down steps to

another picnic table. Turn right onto a forestry track and walk south, high above Loch Long, eventually descending steadily to gain a surfaced road.

Go left along this quiet road, looking out for traffic. This is part of the Cowal Way, Argyll's long-distance walk linking Portavadie on Loch Fyne with Inveruglas on Loch Lomond, some 92km away. Keep left at the junction with the main access road for Coilessan House and follow the road as it continues northwards above Loch Long. After a while, it sweeps left to pass the entrance road of the Ardgartan Hotel, with a view of The Cobbler as you return to Ardgartan car park.

Glen Croe and the Rest and be Thankful

Distance 7.5km Time 2 hours
Terrain forest tracks, old military road
Map OS Explorer 364 Access trains from
Glasgow and Helensburgh to Arrochar;
buses from Arrochar and Helensburgh to
the Rest and be Thankful

Glen Croe runs northwestwards from the
shores of Loch Long to the high point of
the Rest and be Thankful. The glen is
hemmed in by The Cobbler and Beinn
Luibhean to one side, Ben Donich and
The Brack to the other, contributing to
its famously dramatic and sometimes
oppressive feel. This route utilises forest
tracks and a section of old military road.

The Rest and be Thankful sits at 244m
above sea level at the junction of the A83
and the B828 and is overlooked by the
steep crags of Beinn an Lochain. Its name
refers to an inscribed marker stone placed
here by the soldiers who built the original
military road in the mid-1700s. Ever since,
it has provided a welcome break for
drovers, travellers and cyclists who have
taken the steep climb from either Loch
Long or Butterbridge. James Boswell and
Samuel Johnson and Dorothy and William
Wordsworth are just some of the
travellers sufficiently moved to recount
their journeys, though early accounts
were not always flattering. Johnson
described a 'laborious' route in a 'bleak
and dreary region' after his passage
through Glen Croe in the 1770s. In
contrast, after toiling up what Dorothy
described as a 'long, long road' some
30 years later, William Wordsworth
celebrated gaining 'the-wished for Height'
in his sonnet 'Rest and be thankful'.

Today, the military road is free of traffic,
except when the adjacent section of the

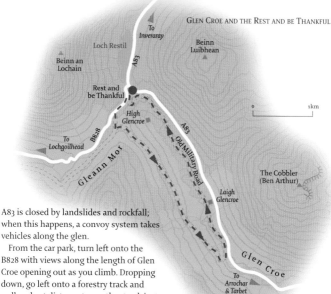

A83 is closed by landslides and rockfall; when this happens, a convoy system takes vehicles along the glen.

From the car park, turn left onto the B828 with views along the length of Glen Croe opening out as you climb. Dropping down, go left onto a forestry track and walk a short distance to another track just before Gleann Mor. Turn left onto this and bear southeast through the forest, high above Glen Croe.

After just under 1km, go left at a fork and descend gradually. For the most part you are above the treeline, with views of the surrounding mountains, particularly The Cobbler. Eventually, after another 2km, the track reaches a bridge on the left, spanning the Croe Water.

Cross this and go left onto the old military road, which was built as part of General Wade's Highland road network and extends for just under 4km to the Rest and be Thankful. Prior to this a simple track existed, one that had been formed by the feet of travellers and the hooves of cattle being driven across

Argyll to the great lowland trysts.

This quiet road travels northwest, initially through conifers, with views opening out to Beinn an Lochain when the trees are left behind. After a stile by a gate, carry on beneath the A83 (opened in 1941 to relieve traffic pressure on the old road) and past the remains of old cottages and sheep fanks.

Another stile marks the start of a steady ascent, which takes you through some wild and impressive scenery – the scale of the landscape dwarfing the old cottage of High Glencroe. A final steep pull zigzags past an old mile marker and the access road of High Glencroe, returning you to the car park.

Beinn an Lochain

Distance 5km Time 4 hours
Terrain hill paths, may be boggy; steep
sections with light scrambling
Map OS Explorer 364 Access trains from
Glasgow and Helensburgh to Arrochar;
buses from Arrochar and Helensburgh
to the Rest and be Thankful, 1.5km from
the start

Of all the Arrochar Alps, perhaps with
the exception of The Cobbler, Beinn an
Lochain has the most mountain character
– with big crags, an airy ridge and several
sections of steep ascent. A little light
scrambling is required, although without
any technical difficulties and there is a
good albeit sometimes boggy path.
With its summit at 901m, however,
care must be taken in poor weather or
winter conditions.

Begin from one of the lay-bys on either
side of the A83, 1.5km north of the Rest

and be Thankful on the Bealach an Easain
Duibh ('the Pass of the Black Water').
A path crosses the Easan Duibh itself
(be prepared for wet feet if the river is
in spate) with a boggy start as it leads
northwest over soft ground towards
a clump of conifer trees. A short steady
climb gains the northeastern tip of
Beinn an Lochain's ridge.

Now curving left, an obvious path rises
southwest – it is a little eroded at points
with several short slabby rocks requiring
both hands and feet. While not
technically difficult at any stage, it slows
progress and care is required, particularly
on the descent.

As you gain height, there are views
eastwards to Beinn Ime's conical outline
and northwestwards to Binnein an
Fhidhleir's spiky ridge on the far side of
Glen Kinglas. Behind you is the Kinglas
Water at Butterbridge, with its historic

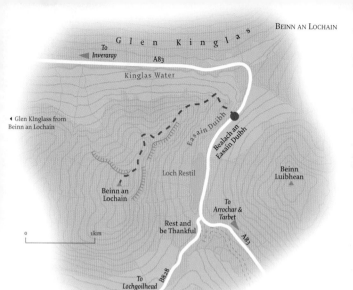

Glen Kinglass from Beinn an Lochain

stone bridge built as part of General Wade's 18th-century military road network.

The path eventually climbs to a flatter section at around the 640m contour line. Ahead rise some very steep crags, which initially look impenetrable. However, the path takes a clear line to the right of these and provides a fairly simple ascent – steep slopes drop down into Glen Kinglas, so a little caution is necessary.

Once around the crags, the path sweeps left and climbs steeply to 750m with a northerly outlook to Ben More, Ben Lui and Ben Oss, all Munros (mountains over 3000 feet/915m), while Loch Restil lies directly below. Beinn an Lochain itself was classified a Munro in Sir Hugh Munro's

original 1891 list, but was later downgraded. With its sharp profile rising above, it's easy to appreciate what a magnificent mountain this is, all the same. Again, the ascent seems tricky but, although steep, it is reasonably straightforward. The path follows a line to the left of steep crags up Beinn an Lochain's eastern face to arrive at the summit cairn with a panorama extending east to the Arrochar Alps and Ben Lomond and northwest to the Cruachan Massif, the Glen Etive Hills beyond and, on a clear day, Mull.

The best way of descent is to carefully return by the outward route, with views all the way.

Ardkinglas wonderland

Distance 3.5km **Time** 1 hour 30
Terrain woodland paths, estate road, hill
to start and steps **Map** OS Explorer 363
Access buses from Glasgow and Oban to
Cairndow road end (north of Cairndow)
on A83, 750m from the start

The designed landscape of Ardkinglas
rises from the banks of Loch Fyne, near the
village of Cairndow. A number of paths
weave through the woodland, home to
several huge tree specimens, a collection
of rhododendrons, varied wildlife and an
old mill. This is a working estate and there
is an admission charge which helps with
the upkeep.

From the entrance, take the woodland
path that passes to the right of the ticket
kiosk. Heading south, it immediately
passes several impressive trees, including
beech and oak dating from the 19th
century. As you gain height, the path is
lined by mountain ash, azaleas and

hydrangeas, before levelling off with
views across the gardens to Loch Fyne.

It is thought that Sir Alexander
Campbell laid out the estate during the
1700s, although there has been an orchard
and culinary garden here since the 14th
century. Exotic conifers from America and
the Far East were planted during the 19th
century by the then Laird, James Henry
Callander, who also established the
pinetum, today home to several of the
garden's Champion trees. Sir Andrew
Noble acquired the site in 1905 and
planted many rhododendrons, with ever-
more exotic species collected by his
successors. After a while, where the path
splits, keep left to walk past a little pond
and on through the woodland to another
fork. Again keep left, signposted for the
Old Mill. The path descends several flights
of steps to cross a footbridge over the
Kinglas Water.

Here, in the depths of this beautiful

‹ Autumn in
Ardkinglas

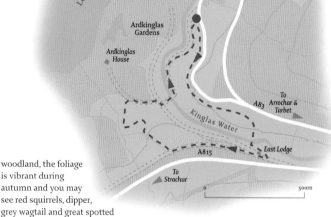

woodland, the foliage
is vibrant during
autumn and you may
see red squirrels, dipper,
grey wagtail and great spotted
woodpecker at various times. The path
sweeps left to reach the remains of the old
grain mill, which dates from the 18th
century. Although a ruin, it is still an
impressive structure.

After passing the mill, the path turns
right and climbs to an estate road. Go
straight across this onto an old road,
beside the octagonal East Lodge, to
continue to the right of the A815.

In 500m, just before the road crosses a
burn, a post marked with a green arrow
points out a path. Turn right onto this
and descend through woodland to a fork.
Go right and carry on along the path as it
swings left and then right before

dropping steadily to a junction near
Ardkinglas House.

Turn right and follow an estate road to a
crossroads, going straight on here to cross
back over the Kinglas Water via a bridge.
After following the road for another 20m,
bear right through a gate onto a
woodland path. This leads past the Grand
Fir – at more than 64m in height, one of
the tallest trees in Britain.

Keep left at a junction, with a
magnificent Silver Fir and a Western Red
Cedar towering above. The path then
passes Sir John's Bank, where some of the
garden's oldest rhododendrons flourish,
and leads back to the car park.

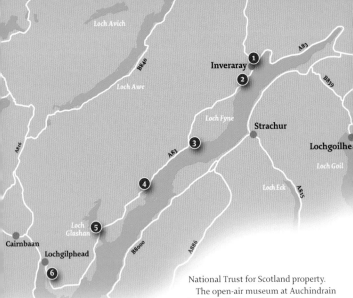

Only a drive of an hour and a half from Glasgow takes you to the popular town of Inveraray, dominated by the distinctive Gothic and Baroque architecture of Inveraray Castle, the ancestral home of the Duke of Argyll and one of Scotland's top visitor attractions.

In this chapter, two walks use estate paths and tracks, away from the hustle and bustle of the castle, including a climb onto the vantage point of Dun na Cuaiche.

Another walk explores Crarae Garden and the Himalayan Glen, where the flowering rhododendrons put on a splendid display in summer. A visit at any time of year is recommended, however, with many plants and trees to see at this National Trust for Scotland property.

The open-air museum at Auchindrain is yet another excellent tourist attraction and just one of the highlights of a walk that begins on the shores of Loch Fyne, climbing through open countryside to a viewpoint and returning through mixed woodland and by the Leacann Water.

Sitting well off the beaten track is Loch Glashan, which has been part of Argyll's hydroelectric scheme since the 1960s. This lonely quarter of Argyll is home to red squirrel, buzzard and butterflies.

Trees, plants and wildlife are also the main attraction in and around Kilmory Woodland on the outskirts of Lochgilphead. Nearby is the 19th-century Kilmory Castle, now the administrative centre for Argyll & Bute Council, who have cared for the woodland and gardens since the 1970s.

Dun na Cuaiche overlooking Loch Fyne ▶

Inveraray to Lochgilphead

Above Inveraray Castle

Distance **6.5km** Time **2 hours**
Terrain **pavement, woodland paths and
tracks, some steep ascents**
Map **OS Explorer 360** Access **buses from
Glasgow and Oban to Inveraray**

**Dun na Cuaiche is the prominent hill that
stands above Inveraray and Loch Shira, an
inlet of Loch Fyne. The climb to the
summit is on good paths, although you
need to tackle a couple of steep sections.
There are sweeping views from the top, as
well as a photogenic folly.**

It was the 3rd Duke of Argyll who made
the decision in 1744 to build a town on the
site of Inveraray village. He commissioned
the renowned architect William Adam to
draw up plans, but it wasn't until the
1770s that the 5th Duke took on the
rebuilding of Inveraray, utilising the
architectural expertise of John Adam and
Robert Mylne.

General Wade's military road, as well as
its location on the west shore of Loch

Fyne, made Inveraray an accessible
destination and it prospered because of
several mills, a herring industry (the town
motto is 'May there always be a herring in
your net') and tourism, which is still the
mainstay of the local economy today.

Facing the pier on Loch Fyne, turn left
and walk alongside the water before
crossing the A83 (which traces the route
of Wade's military road) to follow the
signed entrance drive of Inveraray Castle.
As the drive splits, keep right to head up
to the castle. After admiring the striking
architecture of this Baroque, neo-Gothic
and Palladian building, the drive swings
(left) away from it to pass a monument,
erected in Inveraray in 1754 to
commemorate the execution of 17
prominent Campbells by the 1st Marquis
of Atholl in 1685. The men were all part of
the Covenanter Movement that opposed
King Charles I's attempt to impose a new

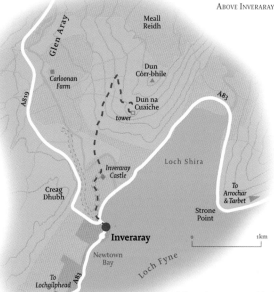

Meall Reidh

Glen Aray

A819

Carloonan Farm

Dun Còrr-bhile

Dun na Cuaiche

A83

tower

Creag Dhubh

Inveraray Castle

Loch Shira

To Arrochar & Tarbet

Inveraray

Strone Point

0   1km

Newtown Bay

Loch Fyne

To Lochgilphead   A83

---

liturgy and prayer book upon the Church of Scotland. It was moved here in 1983 to provide better public access.

Once across the River Aray via an elegant stone arch, known originally as Garden Bridge and built in the mid-18th century by Edinburgh stonemason David Frew, go straight on at a crossroads and bear right onto a blue waymarked path just beyond.

This proceeds through estate woodland, with carpets of bluebells in May, and passes through a gate. Cross a track, then a field before returning to woodland via another gate. This veers right past old limekilns before climbing steadily north to a fork. Take the right branch onto a stony track for a steep ascent with views opening out across Inveraray Estate.

A gradual incline beneath the lower wooded slopes of Dun Corr-bhile follows, before you swing left to climb through a clearing where good views across Loch Shira open out. A series of switchbacks by oak and beech woodland culminates at the 248m summit of Dun na Cuaiche.

The top is marked by a decorative folly built in 1748 by architects Roger Morris and William Adam, who also designed Inveraray Castle. Excavations have uncovered what may be the remains of an Iron Age fort. After enjoying a view that sweeps across Loch Shira, Inveraray and Beinn Ime and Beinn an Lochain, the simplest descent is to retrace your steps.

Inveraray riverside ramble

Distance 10km **Time** 3 hours
Terrain pavement, woodland paths and
tracks **Map** OS Explorer 360 **Access** buses
from Glasgow and Oban to Inveraray

Inveraray Castle is the ancestral home
of the Duke of Argyll and stands proudly
above Loch Shira, an inlet of Loch Fyne.
This walk follows paths and tracks
around the estate and the woodland
surrounding Inveraray.

Facing the pier on Loch Fyne, turn left
and walk alongside the water before
crossing the A83 to follow the signed
entrance drive of Inveraray Castle. As the
drive splits, go right to reach the castle.
The foundation stone of the present-day
structure was laid in 1746, although it took
a further 43 years for this magnificent
building, incorporating Gothic and
Baroque architecture, to be completed.

The castle's architects were Roger
Morris and William Adam who also built
the folly on the summit of Dun na

Cuaiche. Internally, Inveraray Castle is
equally splendid and houses an amazing
array of artefacts, especially the armoury
(open daily April to October). Beyond the
castle and car park, pass the Campbell
Monument, then cross Frew's Bridge
(originally known as Garden Bridge) that
spans the River Aray. The drive continues
for a further 500m before swinging left to
another bridge.

Do not cross; instead bear right onto the
estate road for Carloonan Farm, heading
through countryside to the right of the
River Aray towards the 18th-century
Carloonan Dovecot.

Just before both the doocot and farm,
turn left to cross the Carloonan Bridge,
then go left through a gate and follow
a grassy track downstream, passing
through another gate and crossing an
old bridge.

At a junction, keep right to take the
single-track road past the buildings of
Malt Land, several of which date from the

◄ Inveraray Castle

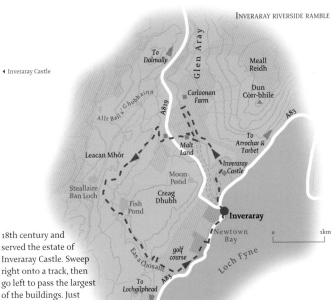

18th century and served the estate of Inveraray Castle. Sweep right onto a track, then go left to pass the largest of the buildings. Just before a wall, turn right and follow a boggy track to reach the A819.

Carefully cross the road onto a rough forestry track beside Electric Cottage. A gentle incline leads to a junction where you go right and cross a bridge over a burn. After rising and falling through dense woodland, the route comes to another junction. Turn left onto Queen's Drive to climb steeply southwest through forest with views across Loch Fyne.

When it drops gently to a fork, keep left to continue through the forest, before swinging left to cross a bridge over a burn, now heading south. After sweeping southeast and descending gradually, you pass a little ruin and a fishpond. Shortly after this, keep straight on to leave the track when it veers left.

An attractive path now drops through mixed woodland, picking up the line of the clear, fast-flowing waters of the Eas a Chosain. When the path ends at a junction, go right onto a narrow road. This sweeps left, then veers left at a fork just before the A83.

A path takes you alongside Inveraray Golf Course. Beyond a gate, follow The Avenue through Newtown, carrying straight on at a junction where a road comes in from the left. After passing the rear of the Loch Fyne Hotel, go right down Barn Brae, a side road, to the A83. Turn left and follow the pavement along the shore of Loch Fyne into Inveraray.

27

Folk trail from Furnace

Distance 10km Time 2 hours 45
Terrain woodland and moorland paths
and tracks, single-track road, some steep
descents and steps Map OS Explorer 360
Access buses from Glasgow to Furnace

This route connects Furnace with the
open-air museum at Auchindrain,
returning by paths through open
countryside and alongside woodland and
riverbanks. Furnace developed during the
18th century and is named after its
historic iron-smelting kilns.

From the war memorial, walk down the
main road past the school and the inn,
and cross the bridge over the Leacann
Water. Turn left onto a narrow road and
head uphill; when it sweeps left, leave the
road to carry straight on along a stony
track through scattered woodland. After a
gate, continue through scenic countryside
with views of the bare summit of Dun
Leacainn which stands above Furnace.

Later, as the track swings right for
South Craleckan, go straight on along a
rougher path into mixed woodland – one
of the most attractive sections of the walk
– before climbing steps out of the woods.
The path continues through a secluded
glen eventually rising to a footbridge.

Cross this, then a low wall, veer left
and walk through birch woodland to
reach a vantage point over the landscape.
A steeper descent using steps takes you
to a junction. Turn left onto a track and
then, just before the A83, go right onto
another path, pass through two gates and
cross a bridge to reach a gate to the left of
Auchindrain Township.

This is thought to be the best surviving
example of a Highland farm township
and, as an open-air museum, provides an
intriguing window into the past (open
daily April to October).

To continue the walk, go through the
gate, carefully cross the A83 and pass

28

◄ Auchindrain Township

through another gate into a field. An indistinct path runs left to a fence and then crosses the field. After a gate, turn left and follow a minor road for 750m. Just before a wooden roadbridge, bear left and cross an old packhorse bridge over Miller's Falls. During the 18th and 19th centuries, this bridge was used by cattle drovers and packhorses transporting charcoal from Loch Awe to Furnace.

Turn left through a gate and drop down past the dramatic waterfall with a path running above the Leacann Water through a beautiful stretch of beech, oak and birch woodland. Eventually the path drops and bears right away from the river. A fenced path then crosses a low wall and turns left through a gate. Carry straight on over a bridge and continue to a track. To the left stands an 18th century double-arched bridge spanning the Leacann Water.

Instead of crossing the bridge, go right and after 20m turn left from the track and cross a footbridge over the Abhainn Dubhan. Beyond a gate, a woodland path continues beside the Leacann Water.

Upon reaching a fork, go right to leave the river behind. Soon after the route sweeps right, take a track on the left. This leads through woodland for 1km before passing through a gate onto a field-edge path. Follow this to its end, then go through a gate and turn left. A rough road leads you back to the A83. Go left onto this, then turn right to return to Furnace.

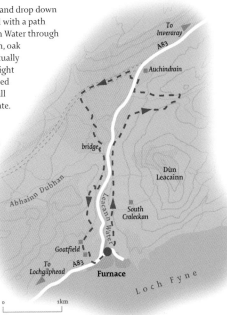

29

Crarae and the Himalayan Glen

Distance 2.5km Time 1 hour
Terrain woodland paths, some with steps
Map OS Explorer 360 Access buses from
Glasgow to Crarae road end on the A83
(request stop only)

Around halfway between Inveraray and
Lochgilphead, Crarae is one of the finest
gardens in Argyll with a huge diversity of
plants and trees, including several
hundred species of rhododendron and an
array of ferns, all helped by the benign
local climate. The National Trust for
Scotland has cared for the garden since
2002 and well-maintained paths run
throughout. The garden is open all year;
admission is free for NTS members.

Crarae began life as a forest garden
more than a century ago. Created in 1912
by Lady Grace Campbell, her son Sir
George Campbell then planted 100 plots
of exotic trees brought back from all
corners of the globe by audacious plant

hunters in the 1930s. His aim was to test
what species could be useful for forestry
in Scotland, and in 1956 he presented the
land to the Forestry Commission who
managed it for more than 20 years.

From the visitor centre, take the path
past a cairn that dates from around
3500BC and was built by the people who
farmed the land here to house the
remains of their ancestors.

At a junction, go left for a gentle climb
up the hillside into woodland, then turn
right onto a track at the next junction.
Identifiable by its red and white
waymarkers, this track leads you past
some of Crarae's famed rhododendron
bushes – *rhododendron* is Greek for 'rose
tree' – to reach a white waymarked path
on the left.

Take this to cross a footbridge and
continue until the path splits. Keep left
here and climb steps leading high above
the glen where native species such as

◄ The Crarae Burn

rowan, birch, oak, Scots pine, willow and ash thrive. Birds you might spot include crossbill, siskin, goshawk and buzzard. At the highest point of the walk, there is a superb view of Loch Fyne.

A short descent regains the main path. Turn left, follow this across a track and continue to the next junction. Turn left (following white and red markers again) and walk beside the Crarae Burn. The glen here is a remnant of the last ice age when glaciers carved out the hanging valley. Steps climb above the river before the path drops down to cross a bridge over it.

Turn left onto a path at a white arrow. This section draws you past specimen

trees such as Chilean Fire Tree and Monkey Puzzle, before dropping down past several impressive eucalyptus trees to another junction. Go right and follow the path past Scots pine.

Take a left at the next junction, then right after a few metres, leaving the white waymarked path behind. Just before the bridge where you crossed the Crarae Burn earlier, turn left onto the red waymarked path for the most dramatic section of the route as it skirts above a series of tumbling waterfalls.

A right turn leads back onto the red and white waymarked path and across another footbridge over the Crarae Burn. Walk left alongside the river and through a little bamboo tunnel. From here, the path continues back to the visitor centre.

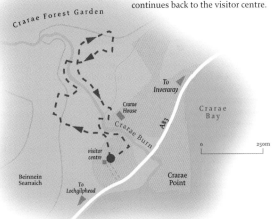

Kilmichael Forest and Loch Glashan

Distance **4km** Time **1 hour 30**
Terrain **forest paths and tracks**
Map **OS Explorer 358** Access **buses from Glasgow to Lochgair, 2km from the start**

Kilmichael Forest sweeps across a rugged landscape of more than 78 sq km to the north of Loch Fyne and Lochgilphead. At its heart lies Loch Glashan, part of Argyll's hydroelectric scheme since the 1960s. Forest paths and tracks cut through this lonely quarter of the region, with plenty of wildlife and views to enjoy throughout.

Start at the Glashan Burn car park, which lies 1km along a forest road, signed off the A83 north of Lochgair. Take the red waymarked path beside the car park which drops downhill into attractive mixed woodland. After veering left, the path runs above an attractive little burn, with much of the woodland floor carpeted with blaeberry. As it rises through the oak, beech and pine woodland, you may spy red squirrels and purple or green hairstreak butterflies at certain times of the year.

When you come to a junction, go left to follow a wide track up to Loch Glashan Dam. Here the track swings left to run beneath the dam wall to another junction. Bear right for a steady climb above Loch Glashan on a surfaced road marked with yellow waymarkers.

Where the road levels off, a waymarked woodland path on the right gives a good optional detour, dropping down to the shores of Loch Glashan, a secluded and picturesque spot with views north along the reservoir.

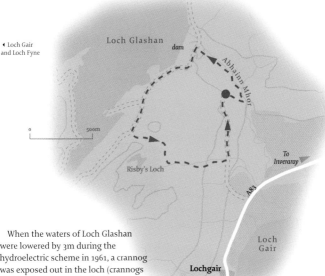

◀ Loch Gair and Loch Fyne

When the waters of Loch Glashan were lowered by 3m during the hydroelectric scheme in 1961, a crannog was exposed out in the loch (crannogs are ancient man-made island structures found predominantly across Scotland and Ireland and used for loch-dwelling). A bronze brooch and Rhineland pottery were also found during excavations, indicating that people lived here around 1500 years ago.

The loch also features in one of Iain Banks' best novels, *The Crow Road*, as does the village of Lochgair, the home of the fictional McHoan family.

Return to the main track to continue southwest. Where the road splits, keep left onto a rougher track, following this for around 100m before bearing left at a waymark onto a grassy path.

This beautiful section takes a sheltered route between pockets of conifer woodland. Another optional detour on the right leads to Risby's Loch where you'll find yourself joined by many dragonflies on a warm summer's day. Continuing the main walk, the path crosses recently cleared hillside with views opening out over Loch Fyne.

After passing an old weir and the remains of a stone building, a gravelly track descends east with Loch Gair and Loch Fyne filling the view ahead and buzzards often circling above.

The steady descent continues to reach the Glashan Burn access road. Turn left and climb along this to return to the car park after 500m.

Kilmory Woodland

Distance 3.25km **Time** 1 hour
Terrain woodland and lochside paths
Map OS Explorer 358 **Access** buses from
Glasgow to Kilmory road end, around
400m from the start

**Sitting on the outskirts of Lochgilphead
is Kilmory Woodland and Castle, the
latter now used by Argyll & Bute Council.
Good paths wander through the tranquil
woodland and along the banks of Kilmory
Loch with plenty of wildlife to see
along the way.**

Kilmory, translating from Gaelic as 'The
Great Church', refers to a church which
once stood here and was held, together
with the surrounding land, by the Abbot
of Paisley in the 1550s. The present-day
castle dates from the 19th century, as do
the grounds, which were laid out in 1830
by William J Hooker, professor of botany

at Glasgow University and at one time
director of Kew Gardens. The many exotic
shrubs and plants that flourished at
Kilmory were said to have matched the
collection held by Edinburgh's Royal
Botanic Garden. After several years of
neglect, the gardens and castle were
acquired by Argyll & Bute Council in 1974
and are today home to a number of rare
trees and shrubs.

From the car park beside Kilmory Castle,
turn left onto the access road before
turning right after a few metres onto a
narrow woodland path. This winds easily
through broadleaf woods to a junction
where you turn right onto a broader track.
Carry straight on at the next junction
before shortly peeling left onto a path
through more attractive woodland.

Beyond a green barrier keep straight on
along a broader track. Turn left at a blue

◀ Kilmory Loch

waymark after 30m to follow a grassy wooded path on a steady ascent – in spring and summer its wildflower borders attract a fleet of butterflies. The gradient soon eases and you come to another junction. Keep right and descend steadily, passing stately beeches, to meet a track.

Turn right here and then left onto a path to reach a bird hide beside Kilmory Loch. You may see great spotted woodpecker and spotted flycatcher during the summer and little grebe, wigeon and teal in the winter. Dragonflies and damselflies are also regular visitors.

With the loch to your right, continue to a fork. Go left through a gap in a wall, where a path now runs along the lochside in a clockwise direction. After a section of boardwalk the path splits again. Go right, climb steps and then walk downhill to cross a burn via stepping stones, returning to the track you left earlier.

Turn left onto this, then left again onto another broad track, which descends to a junction. Go right, continue to the next junction at the back of Kilmory Castle staff car park and turn right. Walk along an access road past another car park, then bear left just before the castle. At a small roundabout, keep right and then left through a gate. A path runs clockwise around the edge of the castle back to its entrance and the start.

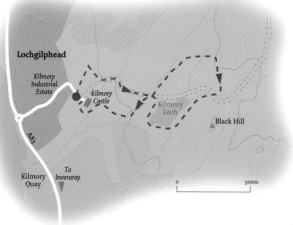

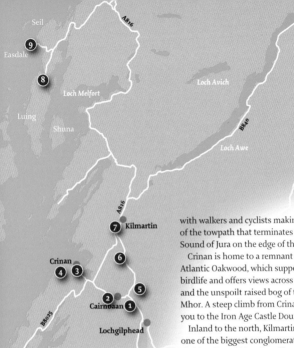

Argyll is bursting with history and nowhere is this more obvious than on the journey north from Lochgilphead.

Whether it is artifacts from the Bronze and Iron Ages or the remains of Argyll's industrial past, history is everywhere.

Cutting a course between Lochgilphead on Loch Fyne and Crinan on the coast is the Crinan Canal, originally devised to save boats the long and arduous journey around the Mull of Kintyre to the Western Isles. Today, pleasurecraft ply the route,

with walkers and cyclists making good use of the towpath that terminates at the Sound of Jura on the edge of the Atlantic.

Crinan is home to a remnant of the great Atlantic Oakwood, which supports much birdlife and offers views across the Sound and the unspoilt raised bog of the Moine Mhor. A steep climb from Crinan also takes you to the Iron Age Castle Dounie.

Inland to the north, Kilmartin Glen holds one of the biggest conglomerations of prehistoric and historic artifacts in Scotland, including burial cairns, rock carvings, stone circles and standing stones. Also found here is the little hill of Dunadd, thought by many to be the birthplace of modern Scotland.

This part of Mid Argyll is home to many idyllic little islands, including Luing and Easdale, two of the Slate Islands named after the dominant slate industry of the 18th and 19th centuries. Although the quarries now lie unused, they offer a fascinating window into the past and are home to much wildlife, while the coastal scenery found here is hard to match.

Crinan from Crinan Oakwoods ▶

Crinan, Kilmartin and the Slate Islands

Crinan Canal towpath

Distance 11.5km **Time** 3 hours (one way)
Terrain pavement, canal towpath
Map OS Explorer 358 **Access** buses to
Lochgilphead; bus from Crinan to
Lochgilphead to return (check timetable
before you set out)

The Crinan Canal linking Ardrishaig on
Loch Fyne with the Sound of Jura at
Crinan is frequently described as 'the
most beautiful shortcut in Scotland'.
Between Lochgilphead and Crinan, the
canal towpath provides an easy and
relaxed linear walk through some of
Scotland's finest scenery.

Lochgilphead was built as a planned
town in 1790 and flourished during the
early 1900s because of its location next to
the Crinan Canal. Over the next 100 years,
it became the administrative centre for
Argyll & Bute, a position still held today.

From the bottom of Argyll Street at
Colchester Square, turn right onto
Poltalloch Street (A83) and walk along the
shores of Loch Gilp, an inlet of Loch Fyne,
with its salty sea air. At the roundabout,
turn left, then almost immediately right
up a slope to the Crinan Canal at Oakfield
Swing Bridge.

Construction of the canal began in 1794
under the guidance of civil engineer John
Rennie. However, problems with the
design and locks meant it was not
completed until 1816 after a major
redesign by Thomas Telford. The canal
granted easier passage for boats between
the Clyde Estuary and Inner Hebrides,
negating the need for a long diversion
around the Kintyre peninsula, and by 1854
it transported 33,000 passengers, 27,000
sheep and 2000 cattle per year.

Passenger services stopped in 1929, but

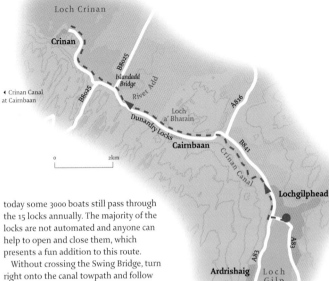

◄ Crinan Canal at Cairnbaan

today some 3000 boats still pass through the 15 locks annually. The majority of the locks are not automated and anyone can help to open and close them, which presents a fun addition to this route.

Without crossing the Swing Bridge, turn right onto the canal towpath and follow this on its journey north and then northwest through a series of picturesque settings. Along the way is plenty of wildlife to look out for, including heron and otter. After around 3km, you come to the attractive village of Cairnbaan, ideal for a break. Turn left through a gap in a wall onto the B841 beside a swing bridge.

Instead of crossing the bridge, go straight on through Cairnbaan along a single-track road. This heads for Dunardry with its series of locks where the canal reaches its highest point of more than 20m above sea level.

Once past Loch a' Bharain and Dunardry Bridge, keep to the towpath at a fork with views opening out across the expanse of the Moine Mhor or 'Great Moss', a National Nature Reserve. At Islandadd Bridge, where the River Add enters the sea, go straight across the B8025 and carry on along the towpath, soon passing the small marina at Bellanoch and, later, a pretty cottage by Crinan Swing Bridge.

The best is yet to come, as the scenic final 1km concludes at the picture-postcard Crinan Basin, where the canal spills out into Loch Crinan and the vista extends across the Sound of Jura and beyond to Mull. To return to Lochgilphead either retrace your steps or make use of the bus.

39

The Dunardry Trail

Distance 5km **Time** 2 hours
Terrain woodland paths and tracks; fairly
steep ascent/descent on An Cruach Mor
Map OS Explorer 358 **Access** buses from
Lochgilphead to Dunardry

The rocky knoll of An Cruach Mor stands
214m above the flat landscape of the
Moine Mhor and the silvery thread of the
Crinan Canal. Most of its slopes are
cloaked in woodland, but its top rises
above the treeline for a panorama that
takes in the many hidden lochs dotting
the forested landscape of Knapdale and
out to sea to the mountainous islands of
Jura and Mull.

The car park sits above the Crinan Canal
just a little east of Dunardry Locks off the
B841. There are views over the canal and
Cairnbaan from here. Exit right from the
car park onto the wide stony access track
and follow this as it rises steadily, passing
through a gate and into larch and spruce
woodland high above the canal. After a

while, pine is replaced by mixed
woodland and you come to a fork.

Keep left to swing southwest, traversing
the lower slopes of An Cruach Mor.
A gentle climb leads out of the woodland
and through a clearing. Where the track
splits again, take the right branch, with
the gradient easing. When it concludes at
a junction, go left onto another track,
which rises gradually to pass the ruins of
several houses.

Shortly afterwards, take a waymarked
path on the left and climb steeply for a
distance of around 250m, emerging above
the treeline to reach the summit of An
Cruach Mor, 'the Great Stack'.

Although little over 200m in height,
there are extensive views from here –
below to the north the River Add snakes
its way through the boggy mattress of the
Moine Mhor and into Loch Crinan, as does
the Crinan Canal, while a number of
lochs, including Loch an Add to the south
and Loch Coille-Bharr to the west, break

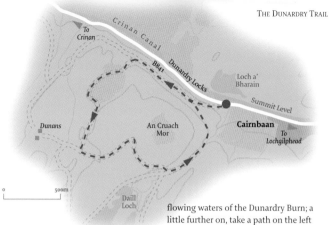

up the woodland of Knapdale. It is the island peaks of Jura and Mull to the west and the angular slopes of Ben Cruachan to the northeast that really draw the eye, however, and it may be hard to drag yourself away on a clear day.

Retrace your steps down to the main track and go left. Another gradual climb follows, after a while becoming a surfaced road which descends to a weir. Bear left, dropping downstream above the fast-flowing waters of the Dunardry Burn; a little further on, take a path on the left which leads back into the trees.

Continuing above the burn, which now tumbles down through a series of waterfalls, the trail passes a distinctive wooden shelter. Ignore a green waymarked path on the right which drops down to the river; instead carry on along the main trail until it splits.

Go left to follow a grassy path with views of the canal. This descends back to the outward track, where you turn right to return to the start.

▼ Loch Crinan from An Cruach Mor

Crinan and the Atlantic Oakwood

Distance 3km **Time** 1 hour 30
Terrain woodland paths, canal towpath
Map OS Explorer 358 **Access** buses from
Lochgilphead to Crinan

Crinan Wood, a remnant of the Atlantic
Oakwood that once extended along much
of Europe's Atlantic Coast, covers the
steep hillside above Crinan. This route
uses a short section of the canal towpath
before climbing through the woodland to
the high point of Dun Mor.

From Crinan Basin car park, take the
path to the left of the basin to Lock 15.
Cross the Crinan Canal as it reaches its
journey's end, flowing into Loch Crinan
and out into the Sound of Jura. Follow a
path past the little Crinan Lighthouse and
then turn left onto the canal towpath at
Lock 14, signposted for Ardrishaig.

Walk southeast along the north bank of
the canal, enjoying views across Loch
Crinan to the 12th-century Duntrune
Castle, thought to be the oldest
continuously inhabited castle in Scotland.
After 750m, with views of the peninsula of
Crinan Ferry across the water to your left,
you come to the 19th-century Crinan
Swing Bridge.

Cross this bridge over the canal,
overlooked by a lovely cottage, and turn
left onto a narrow road. After 20m, take a
flight of rough stone steps on the right
and climb steeply into Crinan Wood.

As a result of the warm, moist gulf-
stream climate, this ancient woodland
(which also includes hazel, ash, rowan,
elm, willow, holly and alder) is home to
an array of lichens, mosses and ferns,
bluebells, blaeberries, foxgloves and
heather, with wildlife that includes red
squirrel, roe deer and 24 species of birds;
redstart, wood warbler and pied flycatcher
being just a few of them. During the 18th

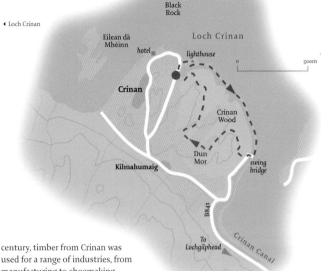

◀ Loch Crinan

Black Rock

Loch Crinan

Eilean dà Mhèinn

hotel

lighthouse

0   500m

Crinan

Crinan Wood

Dun Mor

Kilmahumaig

swing bridge

B841

To Lochgilphead

Crinan Canal

century, timber from Crinan was used for a range of industries, from manufacturing to shoemaking.

After the path swings right, the gradient eases. The trail now meanders up through the woodland to a bench with a view across the Moine Mhor to Dunadd.

In a while, keep left at a waymarked junction and continue on a gradual ascent, eventually emerging above the trees to reach the summit of Dun Mor and sweeping views along the Crinan Canal and the jagged Argyll coastline.

Cross the summit to find a path descending steeply back into woodland before curving right. It now drops more gradually across a little clearing (the small settlement of Kilmahumaig lies below to the left) to a crossroads. Go straight on

and continue to a narrow road.

Go right and walk downhill towards a red-roofed cottage but, just before you reach this, bear left onto a path back into Crinan Wood. This undulates through the woodland to reach the best viewpoint yet, with an outlook that extends across Crinan and the Sound to Jura and Scarba, the eye eventually resting on Mull's mountainous profile.

Bear right and drop steeply down the path back to the Crinan Canal at Lock 14. Do not cross the canal; instead turn left and follow a track the short distance back to the car park.

Castle Dounie from Crinan

Distance **6.25km** Time **3 hours**
Terrain **woodland and hillside paths and
tracks; steep sections** Map **OS Explorer 358**
Access **buses from Lochgilphead to Crinan**

This is a tough walk, with several steep
ascents and descents, following excellent
paths and tracks through the woodland to
the southwest of Crinan. The objective is
a little ridge beneath Creag Mhor to find
the remains of Castle Dounie, an Iron Age
hillfort, and a fantastic viewpoint.

Begin from the small car park that sits
just a little north of Crinan Harbour,
looking out onto Loch Crinan. The village
is best known as the western end of the
Crinan Canal, but it is a great base in its
own right for a variety of outdoor
pursuits, including walking, cycling, sea
kayaking and wildlife watching.

Turn left out of the car park to follow
the narrow shore road past several
houses. As the road swings left, bear right
onto the stony beach and walk along the
shore of Loch Crinan, where oystercatcher,
dunlin, common sandpiper and even otter
may be seen at certain times of the year.
Very shortly, you pick up a path as it
enters oak woodland, clinging to the
coastline as it heads northwest.

A little after crossing a footbridge
over a burn, peel left away from the coast
for a steady climb with a view back down
to Crinan. A steep, prolonged ascent
follows as the path winds up through
woodland to meet a forestry track. Turn
right onto this for a gradual climb to a
fork, where you go left onto the
waymarked 'Forest Walk'.

The track continues beneath steep
craggy slopes. Carry on for almost 500m
and then take a waymarked path on the

◀ Sound of Jura from Castle Dounie

right. After descending through the woods, this then rises steadily alongside craggy outcrops. The path leads to a bench with views stretching west to the many islands dotted along the Sound of Jura and to the mighty Paps of Jura.

Carry on high above the coast to a junction. Turn left here for a long steady climb that rises above the woodland to finally gain the ridge holding the crumbling remains of Castle Dounie. Beyond to the west rise Scarba and Jura and, across the Firth of Lorn, the Isle of Mull, while the view inland sweeps over a large swathe of Argyll's historic landscape.

Retrace your steps from the summit, but then carry straight on at the first junction you come to. The path you are now on drops steeply through woodland (this can be slippery after rain) to eventually pick up another forestry track. Turn right and follow this northeast, before climbing above the headland of Ardnoe Point and then swinging east, high above the coast, with a view out over Loch Crinan.

Keep with the track as it veers sharply left and then returns to the outward route. Go straight on to retrace your steps to Crinan.

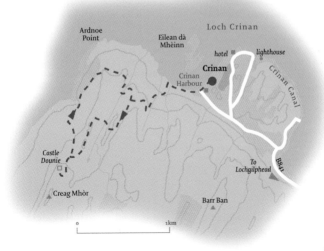

Rings of Achnabreac

Distance 3.25km **Time** 1 hour
Terrain paths and tracks, one short, steep
climb **Map** OS Explorer 358 **Access** no
public transport to the start

The landscape between Lochgilphead and
Kilmartin is littered with an impressive
number of historic sites, not least the cup
and ring markings of Achnabreac. These
carvings provide tangible evidence of the
beliefs and rituals of the communities
who lived here several thousand years
ago. This walk combines two looping
trails around Achnabreac.

Start at the car park that sits 750m east
of the A816 at Cairnbaan. Follow the
yellow waymarked path up a short incline
into a broadleaf wood which is home to
red squirrel, stoat, weasel and deer. It
soon passes the steep slopes of Dun na

Maraig and then climbs sharply to reach
the first group of rock carvings, a complex
design of symbols, spirals, pits and cup
marks with several lines crisscrossing a
large slab of rock – there is also a view of
Loch Fyne from here.

Argyll folklore of the 19th century had
the carvings down as hoof prints until the
antiquarian Sir James Young Simpson
made the first modern analysis of the
area during the mid-1800s. They are
now believed to have been created
around 4500 years ago and are remarkably
similar to designs found along Europe's
Atlantic coast.

Continue along a section of boardwalk
onto a path which rises gently through
woodland to pass another series of 63
carvings, which are thought to have been
fashioned for ritual ceremonies and to

◄ Achnabreac stone carving

communicate with gods and ancestors. In more recent history, the timber of Achnabreac was used during the 17th century for tanning leather while the 1800s saw the oak burnt to make charcoal for Bonawe Iron Furnace.

The path now zigzags up to skirt left of a conifer plantation before levelling off to eventually reach a wide forestry track. Turn left and walk downhill, enjoying views ahead to An Cruach Mor above Dunardry. Carry on along the track until it drops down through a gate, where a left turn then returns you to the car park.

For the second loop in this walk, take the centre of three paths on the right (waymarked red) and follow this over a wooden bridge. The trail veers left through countryside, with boggier ground and scattered woodland on either side – keep your eyes peeled for birds such as coal-, blue- and great-tits, bullfinch, goldcrest and sedge warbler at various times and, in summer, butterflies that include marsh and small pearl-bordered fritillary.

The path curves left to cross a boardwalk before coming to a junction. Turn left here to continue easily back to the car park.

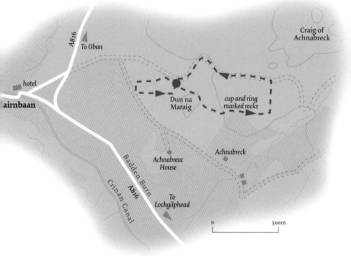

Magical Dunadd

Distance 1.25km **Time** 1 hour
Terrain hill paths, some steep sections
Map OS Explorer 358 **Access** buses from
Oban, Lochgilphead and Ardrishaig to
Dunadd road end

The little rocky hillfort of Dunadd, which
sticks out of the flat mattress bog of the
Moine Mhor, a few miles south of
Kilmartin, is believed to be the capital of
the ancient Gaelic kingdom of Dál Riata.
Although the route to the top is short and
simple, it takes you to the very heart of
Scotland's history.

This walk starts from the car park at the
base of the hill, a short distance off the
A816 between Cairnbaan and Kilmartin.
From here, take the path that climbs

gradually through a gate beside a cottage.

The path soon swings left to traverse
Dunadd's lower craggy slopes. After a
waymark, it takes you uphill with a bit of
clambering over slabs of rock. This is
followed by a flatter grassy terrace where
you can see the remains of the old
ramparts and then a well which supplied
the occupants of the fort with water.
According to legend, the water in the well
once rose and fell with the tide.

Continuing through rocky crags, the
path then veers left to climb steadily onto
the broad grassy summit. Below, the River
Add twists and turns around Dunadd's
base, drawing the eye across the Moine
Mhor and out to sea. It is not hard to see
why the hill was chosen as the site of a

fort as it could be accessed from the sea via the river and any advancing enemy would be easily spotted on the moor.

First occupied in the Iron Age, Dunadd was re-established as a fort by 500AD and soon became the capital of the over-kingdom of Dál Riata which encompassed roughly what is now Argyll and Lochaber in Scotland and County Antrim in Ulster. The people of Dál Riata are often referred to as the *Scotti*, a name first used by Latin chroniclers to describe raiders from Ireland.

Around the summit, look for a footprint and basin carved in stone which are thought to have formed part of the coronation ritual for the kings of Dál Riata. There is also the faint outline of a boar, a symbol of sovereignty, carved in the rock and an inscription in ogham script (an alphabet of straight lines that originated in Ireland) which dates from the late 8th century.

Kings of Dál Riata fought with Picts, Britons, Saxons and each other as power shifted between various factions, until Kenneth MacAlpin, the 36th king of Dál Riata, is thought to have moved the enthroning stone east from Dunadd to Scone, away from Viking raids. Under his reign, the Scots merged with the Picts to form the kingdom of Alba, which eventually became known as Scotland.

There have been several archaeological excavations of Dunadd and many examples of metal-working, including exquisite brooches, have been found. There are also several quern stones, used for grinding corn, dotted around the fort. It is likely that cereals were brought to the kings in their hilltop citadel in tribute.

Return to the start by the same route, taking care over the steeper sections.

◀ Dunadd summit

Kilmartin Glen

Distance 6km **Time** 2 hours 30
Terrain countryside paths, minor roads
Map OS Explorer 358 **Access** buses from
Oban, Lochgilphead and Ardrishaig
to Kilmartin

Kilmartin Glen is home to one of the
richest landscapes of archaeological
monuments in Europe; there are thought
to be more than 350 ancient sites within a
10km radius of the village of Kilmartin.
This walk explores a linear cemetery of
five Neolithic and Bronze Age burial cairns
unique to Scotland, the enigmatic Temple
Wood Stone Circle and the unusually-
aligned Nether Largie Standing Stones
before returning to Kilmartin.

Kilmartin is dominated by its mid-19th-
century church and the kirkyard is home to

a number of sculptured medieval
graveslabs that date from around 900AD to
the 1600s. Stone crosses which originally
stood in the kirkyard are also on display
inside the church, evidence of the area's
long history of Christian worship.

After visiting the excellent Kilmartin
Museum, which puts the sites you will
see on the walk into context, head north
along the A816 and out of the village. Just
before the garage, go through a gate on
the left and cross the field to visit Glebe
Cairn, the first of five burial cairns that
run in a line down Kilmartin Glen.

The Glebe is a typical example of a
burial cairn from the period 1700 to
1500BC. When excavated in the 19th
century two stone cists for burials were
discovered, one of which held a pot

◄ Nether Largie Standing Stones

containing a necklace of jet beads made in Whitby, Yorkshire. Head southwest across the field to cross a bridge over the Kilmartin Burn, then bear southwards to reach Nether Largie North Cairn, which can be entered by sliding back a roof hatch and going down some steps. Look out for the large capstone slab with carvings of axeheads and cup marks. Continue to Nether Largie Mid Cairn, home to two burial chambers and a rare axe-head carving.

At a junction beside the school, bear right onto a minor road and follow this to Nether Largie South Cairn. This is the oldest – centuries older than Stonehenge – and perhaps the most impressive of all the cairns. Burnt bones, pottery, pots, knives, arrowheads and other items found here indicate that it dates from the Stone Age and was rebuilt in the Bronze Age.

The road then leads to the Temple Wood Stone Circle, which stands in an atmospheric pocket of woodland planted in the 19th century by a local landowner. Thirteen of the original 22 stones in the main circle still stand and the remains of a smaller, later circle can be seen nearby.

Continuing, you come to a junction before the houses at Slockavullin. Turn left and follow another minor road before going right along a path to visit Ri Cruin, the last of the five cairns. Return to the road and carry on, before going left at the next junction. When you are opposite a car park, turn left and cross the Kilmartin Burn by a bridge to visit the X-shaped Nether Largie Standing Stones. Thought to have been erected some 3200 years ago, the tallest stone is around 3m high. Four of the stones are aligned with the burial cairns, with the fifth stone sitting at the centre of the cross.

Head northwest across the field and go through a gate beside a small wood. A fenced path leads back to Nether Largie South Cairn and from there you can retrace your steps to Kilmartin.

Cuan Sound and Cullipool

Distance 6.75km **Time** 2 hours
Terrain coastal paths, one short awkward
section of beach (check tide times before
you go), minor roads **Map** OS Explorer 359
Access bus from Oban to North Cuan on
Seil; daily ferry sailings from here to
South Cuan on Luing

The beautiful Slate Island of Luing is
separated from Seil by the narrow Cuan
Sound. Its history as a major producer of
slate is evident on this walk which visits
the island's main settlement of Cullipool.
Agriculture has also been important here
and the Luing breed of cattle was officially
recognised by the British government in
1965. The coastal paths are good, although
there is one awkward beach section which
may be impassable in very high tides.

The island is reached by a three-minute
ferry journey from North Cuan on the Isle
of Seil which, in turn, is accessed by road
via the humble single-arch 'Bridge over
the Atlantic'. From the ferry slipway on
Luing, turn right onto a track just before
the small ferryman's hut and follow this
along the coast. Beyond a gate, continue
northwest along a grassy path with views
of Easdale and Ellenabeich; here in
summer, you may spot black guillemot
and common tern.

As the path rounds Cuan Point, you'll
see the first reminders of the slate
industry, including stone workhouses and
a flooded pit where dark green waters
reflect the quarried cliffs above.

A grassy track now heads south along
Luing's western fringes looking out to the
'Rough Islands' of the Garvellachs, more
evocatively known as 'the Isles of the Sea',
and the tiny island of Fladda with its
lighthouse. After curving round the scenic

◀ Torsa and Seil from Luing

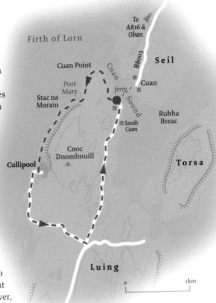

Port Mary, the track splits. Go right onto a path which continues beneath steep cliffs up to the left. At times it can be wet, but you soon reach the large fin of Stac na Morain jutting out from the cliffs. Cross this via a stile at its left edge.

The grassy path continues in the shadow of the steep embankment, then just before a rocky outcrop it veers right towards the shore. A narrow, bouldery stretch of beach now has to be negotiated. Awkward but short-lived this may, however, be impassable at very high tides.

From here, a good track proceeds along a grassy cliff-lined terrace to Cullipool where a road leads on through this lovely coastal village; birds to look out for include redshank, oystercatcher and, depending on season, turnstone and ringed plover.

For 200 years during the 18th and 19th centuries, Cullipool was the centre of the slate industry on Luing and, at its height, employed more than 150 men. Having extracted the slate, it was then passed by hand along a line of men, loaded onto boats and shipped all over Scotland.

Where the road splits, keep right and walk out of the village along the coast, passing the old harbour with views of Scarba and Lunga. In a while, the road swings inland, passing several houses and the village store and post office.

At a T-junction, turn left past Luing Fire Station to follow the road north, rising gently through pleasant countryside before a gradual descent with views of Torsa, the Cuan Sound and Seil. An easy final 1.5km takes you back to South Cuan.

An Easdale round

Distance 2km Time 1 hour Terrain coastal and hill paths; one steady ascent and descent, exposed section around quarry Map OS Explorer 359 Access bus from Oban to Ellenabeich; daily ferry sailings from here to Easdale

Easdale is the smallest Slate Island with a permanent population. Fascinating and scenic in equal measure, this walk around the island that was once at the heart of the Scottish slate industry has plenty of history to unearth – but it is the view from High Hill that is likely to provide the most enduring memory.

Traffic-free Easdale is easily reached by taking the regular passenger boat from Ellenabeich on the western edge of Seil across the 200m-wide Easdale Sound. After disembarking, turn right onto a track and walk through the village, passing a number of whitewashed

terraced cottages, the contemporary community hall and an excellent pub. The Easdale Museum is signposted to the left and is well worth a visit (open daily from March to October).

For 300 years from the early 17th century, Easdale was at the heart of Argyll's slate industry, employing hundreds of people during its 19th-century heyday. However, a massive storm in 1881 flooded many of the quarry pits that are still visible today, hastening the demise of the industry – although it held on until the 1950s.

During the 1960s, the island had a population of just four, but today it boasts a thriving community of almost 70. Tourism is the mainstay of Easdale's economy with the World Stone Skimming Championships, which draw hundreds of competitors and big crowds every year, a particular highlight. The event takes place on the last Sunday of September. If you

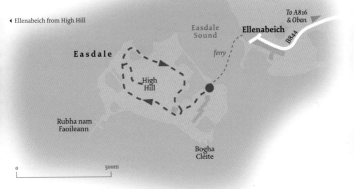

◄ Ellenabeich from High Hill

Ellenabeich

Easdale Sound

To A816 & Oban

B844

ferry

Easdale

High Hill

Rubha nam Faoileann

Bogha Cleite

0   500m

have a bit of time between ferries, Easdale is the place to perfect your skimming technique, with plenty of raw material at your disposal.

After the track swings right, take another track on the left. This splits after a few metres. Keep right and then right at the next fork to follow a path which runs between buckthorn and bramble bushes. The sharp fin of High Hill rises to the right and views open out towards Mull. The trail soon curves right and passes the remains of two slate workhouses.

Just before the third of these, turn right onto a narrow path and follow this as it climbs steadily up the heather-clad slopes of High Hill – at 38m, the highest point of the island. The incline eases as the path sweeps right and then left to gain the viewpoint indicator on the summit.

As well as offering views of Easdale and Seil, this spot gives a fine outlook across

the islands, including Mull, Lismore, Scarba, Luing and even Colonsay, and down to the Mull of Kintyre.

Walk back down to the main path, turn right and continue above the coast. Swinging right, the trail makes its way above two flooded quarry pits with stunning turquoise waters where guillemot, cormorant and common tern can sometimes be spotted. There is a steep drop either side into the pools, so care is needed here.

The path leads back towards the village, past the remains of the quarries and workhouses which nature is beginning to recolonise, with bramble, clover, ferns and heather taking root and covering the slate deposits.

At a junction, keep right onto a stony track beside the harbour and follow this back into the village, retracing your steps to the ferry.

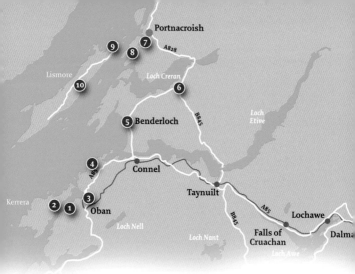

Oban is the largest settlement in this region – a bustling town with fine shops, pubs and restaurants, particularly seafood for which it is renowned. The focal point of the town is its harbour, overlooked by McCaig's Tower, and to really get your bearings, an excellent walk visits both.

Another good look-out point is Pulpit Hill where you can watch the many ferries ply their course from the 'Gateway to the Isles' towards their Hebridean destinations.

Just off the coast of Oban is Kerrera, an island with a wild and remote feel, particularly along its western side with its outlook to Mull. Kerrera is also home to the historic Gylen Castle, a MacDougall stronghold when built in the 16th century.

An earlier MacDougall fortress is Dunstaffnage Castle, which was built around 1220. It is reached from Ganavan Bay by a ruggedly picturesque stretch of coastline and a hike over Ganavan Hill.

North of Oban is Sutherland's Grove where impressive trees and plenty of chances to spot wildlife are highlights of a walk. Beinn Lora, above the village of Benderloch, meanwhile, is a perfect vantage point for surveying much of Argyll, including Ben Cruachan, Loch Etive and the Lynn of Lorn National Scenic Area.

Situated at the point where Loch Linnhe and Loch Etive meet the Sound of Mull, the Lynn contains an array of limestone islets against a wild and rocky mountain backdrop. Four walks explore different corners of the National Scenic Area – Port Appin and the striking rock arch of Clach Thoull, the fertile, low-lying 'Great Garden' of the Isle of Lismore, and brooding loch-bound Castle Stalker, one of Argyll's most iconic historic structures with an intriguing past.

Oban to Appin

Beyond Pulpit Hill

Distance 7.5km **Time** 2 hours
Terrain pavement, paths, minor road
Map OS Explorer 359 **Access** Oban is well
served by buses and trains

Oban is the main port for the Hebrides
and one of the major settlements along
Scotland's west coast. It's a busy place
and was once dubbed 'the Charing Cross
of the Highlands', but there are many
quieter spots nearby, as you can discover
on this walk to the viewpoint of Pulpit
Hill and the hillfort of Dun Uabairtich
overlooking the Sound of Kerrera.

From Oban Harbour follow Station
Road to Argyll Square, then go right
along Albany Street away from the town
centre. After the road crosses a railway
line, keep left at a fork signposted for
Pulpit Hill.

Head up to a junction and then follow
Haggart's Brae to reach Glenmore Road.
Turn right and when the road forks take
the right branch to rejoin Glenmore Road
at its junction with Villa Road. Carry on
for a short distance to a path which
climbs to the top of Pulpit Hill.

At the summit, a viewpoint indicator
sets out what you can see and to the east
of it is the Minister's Stone on which the
minister was said to have stood to
deliver his sermons.

Walk through a car park, passing
public toilets, and go down Pulpit Hill
Road and then Pulpit Drive. After a few
metres, turn left onto the track
signposted for Kerrera Ferry. It travels
through a pocket of woodland and then
narrows to a path as it heads out into
quiet, open countryside.

Go through several gates as you head
southwest above Ardbhan Craigs; in

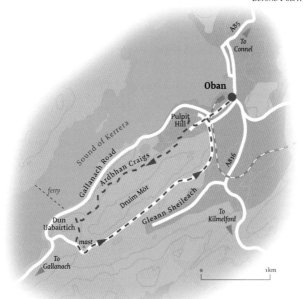

spring and summer this is home to meadow pipit, wheatear, scatterings of wildflowers and an abundance of butterflies. In a while, the path splits. Keep left (right leads down to the Kerrera Ferry) and follow the narrow path up through bracken-covered hillside, enjoying the view along the Sound of Kerrera and the Firth of Lorn and out to the islands of Kerrera and Mull.

When the path runs between two embankments, watch closely for it forking. Take the right branch and climb gradually to the Iron Age fort of Dun Uabairtich, another fine vantage point.

Go down its southern slope and pick up a vague path that drops steeply to a fence beside a cottage. Walk right and, once through a gate, turn left onto the minor Glenshellach Road (a right turn leads to the small settlement of Gallanach) which climbs through tranquil countryside and past a television mast.

The road then veers left and continues easily northeast through Gleann Sheileach for around 2.5km back to Oban. At a junction, go left onto Glenmore Road and walk back to Haggart's Brae. Turn right and drop down to Albany Street, then retrace your steps to Oban Harbour.

◀ The Sound of Kerrera

A Kerrera horseshoe

Distance 11km **Time** 3 hours **Terrain** minor road, coastal path **Map** OS Explorer 359 **Access** Oban is well served by buses and trains; limited weekdays-only bus from Oban to the Gallanach Road slipway with its small car park. Frequent daily sailings from here to Kerrera

To step onto Kerrera is to step back in time. A short ferry journey takes you into a tranquil, bygone world – unless you live on Kerrera no vehicles are allowed, so a peaceful walk is guaranteed. The wildlife adds considerably to the route's appeal, but there are also memorable views, especially of Mull and Ben Cruachan.

After disembarking from the ferry, follow the rough single-track road to a phonebox. Bear left and at a fork keep left again. The road heads southwest around Horseshoe Bay where on 8 July 1249 King Alexander II died as he waited to mobilise the army that he hoped would lead to the defeat of King Haakon and the reclamation of the Western Isles from Norway.

Once around Little Horseshoe Bay, the road climbs steeply past several ruined cottages at Upper Gylen before dropping steadily through peaceful countryside towards Lower Gylen. Beyond a gate, walk downhill towards Kerrera Tea Garden and Bunkhouse (open daily Easter to September) but, just before this, turn left through a gate for Gylen Castle.

A grassy path crosses a field, then goes through rocky outcrops (keep an eye out for wild goats) to reach the castle's dramatic remains, a MacDougall stronghold when built in around 1582. Its walls used to hold the Brooch of Lorn, which is one of the most important items

in Scottish history as it is said to have been ripped from the breast of Robert the Bruce during the Battle of Dalrigh in 1306. The celebrated artist J M W Turner visited here in 1831, filling his sketchbook with drawings of Gylen Castle.

Retrace your steps to the road, turn left, walk past the tearoom (or pop in for a cuppa if open) and continue towards Kerrera's rugged western end where there are terrific views of Mull. Upon reaching Port Dubh, a grassy track climbs past a house at Ardmore.

After this, a rough path bears north along the island's remoter western edge beneath the slopes of Torbhain Mor with views of Lismore to reach the hushed beauty of Barr-nam-boc Bay.

During the 18th and 19th centuries, drovers landed their cattle here from Mull, Coll and Tiree. At Ardantrive Bay on the northern tip of Kerrera, the cattle would swim to the mainland (*Ardantrive* means 'Point of the Swimming') and onwards to major trysts at Falkirk and Crieff.

The path broadens to a single-track road, leading past a cottage and the remains of a settlement. A steep climb takes you northeast away from the sea with views of the top of Ben Cruachan, Oban and the Argyll coastline. The road meanders high above the coast before descending through a few gates. Nearing the ferry terminal, pass an old church and several cottages, then fork right to return to Horseshoe Bay. Turn left back to the slipway.

◀ Ben Cruachan from Kerrera

Oban and McCaig's Tower

Distance 2.5km **Time** 1 hour
Terrain pavement with some steep climbs
Map OS Explorer 359 **Access** Oban is well
served by buses and trains

Sitting high above Oban town centre on
Battery Hill is McCaig's Tower, which for
more than a century has been an ideal
vantage point for surveying Oban and its
coastline. As well as soaking up the views,
this simple route takes in the town's
harbour and distillery.

The humble origins of Oban's name –
translating from Gaelic as 'Little Bay' or, in
full, 'the Little Bay of Lorn' – belie its
position both as Scotland's Seafood
Capital and as the Gateway to the Isles,
with many ferries leaving here for
Lismore, Mull, Coll, Tiree, Barra and South
Uist amongst other islands. A major
tourist destination since the railway

arrived in the 1880s, Oban Harbour still
has a small fishing fleet and the bay sees a
lot of traffic, from large ferries and yachts
to fishing trawlers and pleasurecraft.

From the harbour, follow Station Road
to Argyll Square, then walk left along
Aird's Place and George Street to
Stevenson Street. Turn right, then bear
left onto Hill Street, signposted for
McCaig's Tower. This climbs steeply (there
is no pavement so be aware of traffic),
sweeping right and then left past some
handsome stone villas.

Follow Rockfield Road, then turn left to
take Ardconnel Road, before turning right
onto Duncraggan Road beneath McCaig's
Tower. After 30m, bear left to follow a
path to the coliseum-like structure. The
viewing platform enables you to look out
over Oban to Kerrera, to Lismore's white
lighthouse and across the Firth of Lorn to

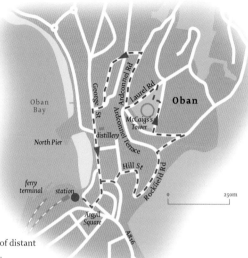

Mull with its jumble of distant peaks on the horizon.

The tower was commissioned by, and subsequently named after, Oban banker John Stuart McCaig, partly as a means of employing local stonemasons – who had little work during the winter – and to house a museum and art gallery.

Construction began in 1895 with the intention for it to be an enclosed building. However, McCaig's death in 1902 meant the money for its completion was not available and only the outer walls were ever built.

Retrace your route along the path and go down some steps on the left through a car park onto Laurel Road. Turn left and follow this quiet street downhill past several attractive cottages.

At Ardconnel Road, turn right before curving left onto Dalriach Park Terrace to reach a crossroads. Keep straight on and drop down the narrow Albert Road (this is a one-way street so keep an eye out for oncoming traffic) onto Craigard Road and then George Street in Oban town centre.

Go left, then left again to reach Oban Distillery, impossible to miss with its distinctive red and black chimney. Whisky distilling began here in 1794 and today the distillery welcomes more than 35,000 visitors a year. Return along Oban's attractive seafront to the start.

◀ Oban Harbour and McCaig's Tower

Coast trail to Dunstaffnage

Distance 6.5km **Time** 2 hours 30 (round trip) **Terrain** rough coastal, hill and woodland paths; some steep ascent **Map** OS Explorer 359 **Access** buses from Oban to Ganavan Bay

A rugged stretch of coastline extends from Ganavan Bay, 3km north of Oban, and across Ganavan Hill with its panoramic views to reach the impressive castle at Dunstaffnage Bay. At times, the paths can be rough underfoot and there are a couple of steep ascents on this tough but fulfilling walk.

Ganavan Bay is a popular spot, with its sandy beach and scenic location. Walk north from the car park along a seawall and, once up some steps, a rough coastal path passes through a gate and continues northeast with views of Lismore and the mountains on the distant Morvern peninsula. It then proceeds under steep cliffs and, after 1km, comes to a junction beneath a gully.

Turn right and ascend a steep narrow path onto the clifftop. Go left to follow a high-level grassy path northeast to a three-way split. Take the right path for a short ascent onto Ganavan Hill with its views southwest down to Kerrera, inland to the immense peak of Ben Cruachan and northwards to Beinn a'Bheithir.

Descend Ganavan Hill and, after passing through a gap in a fence, bear left and drop down a steep, rough path which swings right beneath more cliffs and along the rocky coast – you may spot black guillemot and ringed plover along the shoreline here.

Beyond the cliffs, continue across coastal grassland where the path can be indistinct – if in doubt, stick to the shore. In a while, you cross a low fence and now an obvious path heads around the inlet of Camas Rubha na Liathaig to a junction.

Turn left and walk past the Scottish Marine Institute (its Ocean Explorer Centre is open to visitors) into attractive

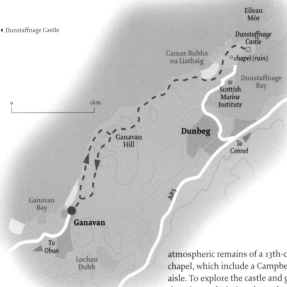

◄ Dunstaffnage Castle

woodland. Continue to Dunstaffnage Castle, beautifully positioned overlooking Dunstaffnage Bay. It has had a turbulent history since being built by the MacDougalls around 1220. It was involved in the Wars of Independence (1296–1356) and the dispute between Scotland and Norway for control of the Western Isles, and was attacked by Robert the Bruce in 1308 after his famous victory over the MacDougalls at the Pass of Brander. It fell into the hands of Clan Campbell during the 15th century.

Within the woodland are the atmospheric remains of a 13th-century chapel, which include a Campbell burial aisle. To explore the castle and grounds, there is an admission charge but it is well worth a visit (open daily in spring and summer and from Sunday to Wednesday in winter).

Retrace your steps beyond Ganavan Hill and southwest along the clifftop as far as the gully. However, instead of going back down this, carry straight on here and keep your height – before long Ganavan Bay's arc of sand comes back into view. The grassy clifftop is an ideal place to sit and watch the ferries sailing between Oban, Mull and Lismore.

The path descends through gorse before veering right back to the outward path. Turn left and return to Ganavan Bay.

Beinn Lora

Distance 6km **Time** 2 hours 30
Terrain woodland and hill paths. Some
steep sections; navigation skills required
Map OS Explorer 376 **Access** buses from
Oban and Fort William to Benderloch

Rising to 308m above the village of
Benderloch, a few miles north of Connel,
Beinn Lora is a good place to survey much
of the Argyll landscape and the West
Highlands. Excellent paths line the
majority of the walk, but around 1km
before the summit a rougher path, at
times indistinct and boggy, continues –
good navigation is required here
if visibility is poor.

From the Beinn Lora car park at the
southern end of the busy village of
Benderloch, go through a gate and bear
right when the path splits. A steep climb
takes you quickly above Benderloch,
following red/blue waymarks, with good
views opening out across the Firth of
Lorn. Several steep sections persist
through attractive woodland where
you may see red squirrels and hear
woodpeckers. When the path swings
left, the incline eases a little and you
eventually reach a junction just after
a viewpoint.

Turn right (blue/red waymark) for a
steady climb, with the path zigzagging up
to emerge above the treeline – a couple of
picnic tables and benches bring a little
relief from the ascent with a view across
Ardmucknish Bay to Rubha Garbh-aird,
sweeping southwards to Dunstaffnage
Bay, Kerrera and Mull.

At a junction, turn right (a short detour
left gains the Eagle's Eyrie and a view
north) to follow a wide track along an
easy gradient to a three-way split. Take

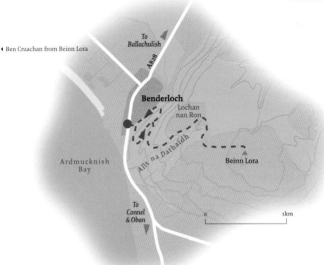

◀ Ben Cruachan from Beinn Lora

To Ballachulish

A828

Benderloch

Lochan nan Ron

Allt na Dathaidh

Ardmucknish Bay

Beinn Lora

To Connel & Oban

0 — 1km

the central path and follow this around a peaceful wetland area, filled with bogcotton, common spotted orchid, butterflies and dragonflies during the summer. The path then climbs to a picnic table beside a gate. Here, the blue trail ends, though in clear weather the craggy top of Beinn Lora can be spied ahead.

To continue on a more adventurous footing, go through the gate onto a rougher path which drops down to a flatter grassy area – this can be boggy after periods of rain. Any difficulties are short-lived and, beyond, a stony path climbs steadily east. After another brief boggy section, where the path is again a little indistinct, the going improves as it crosses firmer ground. A steep final pull leads up onto Beinn Lora with its rewarding views. Loch Etive draws the eye to Ben Cruachan's distinctive profile, with Ben Lui and the Arrochar Alps rising beyond. The Glen Coe and Glen Etive mountains climb sharply to the north, while Morvern and Ardgour create an impressive barricade to the west. On a clear day, the view south sees the Paps of Jura emerge from the sea.

Walk back down to the blue trail, retracing your steps from here to the blue/red waymark. Here, turn right and drop down through pleasant woodland. At times the descent is steep, but when the path sweeps sharply left it eases for a gentle walk back to the start.

Sutherland's Grove

Distance 5km **Time** 1 hour 30
Terrain waymarked paths and tracks
Map OS Explorer 376 **Access** buses from
Oban and Fort William to Barcaldine

This scenic trail follows well-maintained
woodland paths and the course of the
dramatic Abhainn Teithil to reach the
secluded Gleann Dubh Reservoir. Peace
and quiet reign as the route returns to
the start via a magnificent viewpoint.
The walk is waymarked.

The start point is a small car park that
sits 100m off the eastern side of the A828
just north of Barcaldine. Do not cross the
old stone bridge that spans the Abhainn
Teithil; instead take the path just before it,
waymarked for all routes. A riverbank trail
makes its way through Sutherland's Grove

where several Douglas Firs, planted in
1870, now stand more than 30m in height.

The grove is named after Lord
Sutherland who was the President of the
Society of Foresters and helped set up the
Forestry Commission in 1919. Many more
trees were planted here in 1921 in his
honour, and the woodland also contains
birch, beech, rowan and oak.

A gradual incline soon turns to a steady
climb east above a spectacular wooded
gorge, where a series of waterfalls have
shaped the rocks into some striking
shapes. Within the woods and along the
river, wren, treecreeper and dipper are
frequent visitors.

Continue to climb to a junction beside a
bridge. Do not cross it, but instead turn
left away from the Abhainn Teithil, then

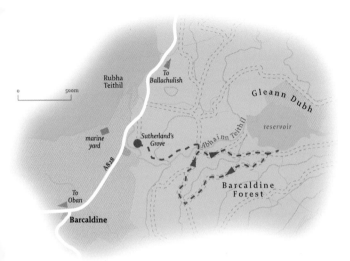

immediately fork right. An easy section of path, following green and red waymarks, continues alongside the now more gentle flow of the river.

At another junction, turn right via green waymarks and cross a bridge over the river onto a wide forest track. When this splits, go left and walk uphill through conifers where you may hear the rat-tat-tat of the great spotted woodpecker. After a while, the track forks again; stay right to keep climbing gradually.

On levelling off, go left onto another track that comes in from the right, then bear left onto a path and drop a short distance to the shores of Gleann Dubh Reservoir – a picnic bench makes this a good choice for a break.

Retrace your steps to the main forest track, going right and then left when it forks, and continue to walk along the forest drive.After around 1km, this takes you to a track on the right. Follow this to arrive at a viewpoint after a few metres; the outlook extends across Loch Creran and Loch Linnhe to the mountains of the Morvern Peninsula and Mull.

The track now descends and, in due course, a blue waymarked route joins from the left. Carry on down to a junction where you bear left to walk back over the bridge crossed earlier before turning left onto the outward path. Retrace your steps down through the Abhainn Teithil's dramatic gorge and back to the start.

◀ Loch Creran from Sutherland's Grove

Castle Stalker outlook

Distance 4km Time 1 hour 30 (including detour) Terrain minor road, cycle/walkway Map OS Explorer 376 Access buses from Oban and Fort William to Appin

Castle Stalker is one of Argyll's most popular and iconic structures. It holds a commanding position at the point where Loch Laich joins Loch Linnhe near the village of Appin. The recently refurbished Jubilee Bridge spans the mudflats at the head of Loch Laich, creating a circular walk rich in history, scenery and wildlife.

From the large car park opposite Appin Village Hall, turn right and follow the pavement beside the A828 through the village. Meaning 'Abbey Lands', Appin refers to the land owned by the medieval abbey on Lismore, founded by St Moluag, the Patron Saint of Argyll.

Turn left onto a minor road for Port Appin and follow this west. Lined with birch and rowan trees, it gives brief glimpses of Castle Stalker.

After 1.25km, turn right onto a surfaced path, signposted for the Jubilee Bridge, and follow this alongside Loch Laich, an inlet of Loch Linnhe. Because of its saltmarsh, mudflats and rich grassland habitats, this is an important area for birdlife, including oystercatcher, Canada goose, ringed plover, lapwing, turnstone, sandpiper and snipe; otter, water vole and grey seals can also be found here.

The wooden Jubilee Bridge was built in 1898 to provide better access to the local Free Church for those living in Portnacroish. Prior to this, crossings were made by horse and cart while livestock were moved along a waymarked route at low tide. The bridge was also apparently useful for the local postman.

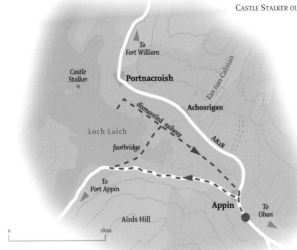

As you make the crossing, Castle Stalker stands prominently on its own island on Loch Linnhe, although its outline is dwarfed by the massive mountains of Kingairloch on the horizon.

Translating from the Gaelic *Stalcaire* as either 'Hunter' or 'Falconer', Castle Stalker was constructed by Clan MacDougall in around 1320 with its present guise built by Lord Stewart of Lorn in the 15th century. A Stewart stronghold for more than 200 years, it was bizarrely lost in 1620 in a drunken wager with the Campbells of Airds.

The Stewarts regained Castle Stalker in 1689 but lost it that same year after a defeat at the Battle of Dunkeld, and it withstood the Stewart cannonballs during the 1745 Jacobite Uprising. Slightly less seriously, the castle had a small role

playing the Castle of Aaargh! in the movie *Monty Python and the Holy Grail*. (The castle is accessible only by pre-booked tour subject to season, weather and tide times.)

On the far side, a section of boardwalk joins a path which then culminates at a cycle/ walkway. For an enjoyable detour, turn left, cross a bridge over a burn and continue easily for 500m to a minor road at Portnacroish. Turn left and take a track onto a stony beach. Here, at lower tides, you can get a little closer to Castle Stalker without risking wet feet.

Retrace your steps to the bridge on the cycle/walkway but now carry straight on, heading southeast towards Appin. This attractive path is lined with rowan, oak and birch and, after 1km, concludes at the A828. Turn right and follow the pavement back into Appin.

◀ Castle Stalker across Loch Laich

Port Appin to Clach Thoull

Distance 2.5km **Time** 1 hour
Terrain coastal track, minor road
Map OS Explorer 376 **Access** there is no
public transport to Port Appin

Port Appin sits a little off the beaten track
at the end of a single-track road by the
shores of Loch Linnhe. It is a popular
destination, especially for those wishing
to take the short ferry journey to Lismore.
There are plenty of other reasons to visit,
however, including some intriguing
geology and wonderful flora and fauna, as
illustrated in this simple, attractive walk.

Port Appin, reached via a minor road off
the A838 at Appin, has a post office,
community shop and hotel, as well as
picturesque views across the Lynn of Lorn
to Lismore. There is a car park behind the
hotel and limited parking beside the
harbour slipway.

From the harbour look for the
signposted 'Public Footpath to Clach
Thoull'. Follow this past the car park and
onto a rougher track which leads past
several houses. After the last house, the
track runs southwest beneath steep
cliffs cloaked in woodland, including
Scots pine and rowan.

Beyond a gate carry on along the track,
itself lined with ash, sycamore, birch and
rowan, while bluebell, yellow pimpernel,
bugle, bilberry and greater stitchwort are
just a few of the wildflowers to look out
for in spring and summer. After 750m, it
swings left past a bench to approach the
natural rock arch of Clach Thoull.

Just before this, it is worth taking a path
on the right down to the headland where
the view southwest along the Lynn of
Lorn extends past Lismore to Kerrera and,
on a clear day, to the island chain of the

◄ Loch Linnhe from Port Appin

Eilean
nan Caorach

Rubh Àird
Ghainimh

Inn
Island

To
Appin

ferry

Lismore

jetty

Port Appin

Lynn of Lorn

Appin
Rocks

Clach
Thoull

Airds
Bay

Airds
Point

0   1km

Garvellachs. Dun da Ghaoithe and Ben More on Mull are also visible. Sightings of otter and seal are possible, while regular visitors include ringed plover, oystercatcher and, during the winter, turnstone. Sea pinks, lesser sea spurrey and common scurvy grass are just a few of the coastal wildflowers that can be found here.

Return to the main track and carry on along this. You can either walk past or take the path through the impressive Clach Thoull (simply translating from Gaelic as 'Hole in the Rock') and continue around the headland, turning northeast alongside Airds Bay, which at low tide is popular with birdwatchers. With steep wooded crags rising to the left of the path and views of the mountains of Glencoe and Glen Etive, this is a picturesque section of the walk.

At the head of Airds Bay, you come to a beautifully situated house. Bear left through a gate to the right of the house onto a woodland path signposted for Port Appin; birch, oak, hawthorn, ash, rowan, willow, holly and sycamore populate the woodland, a habitat well liked by wood

and willow warbler and chiffchaff.

The path is easily followed for 250m. Once through a gate, turn left onto a minor road and, after just a few metres, go left again onto another small road, signposted for the Lismore Ferry. This takes you back into Port Appin.

Pass the village hall and adjacent lighthouse lantern, the unusual home of a local history exhibition, continuing as the road sweeps left past the community co-op back to the harbour.

Lismore Point to Port Ramsay

Distance 4.25km Time 1 hour 30
Terrain coastal paths, minor roads
Map OS Explorer 376 Access there is no
public transport to Port Appin; regular
daily sailings from Port Appin to Lismore

Lismore is an idyllic island on Loch Linnhe,
lying just a short distance across the Lynn
of Lorn from Port Appin. As with Kerrera,
a short passenger ferry journey (bikes are
also allowed) transports you into a more
peaceful, laid-back world. A lovely little
walk leaves from Point, where the ferry
docks, and follows the coast to Port
Ramsay Bay before quiet roads lead back
to the slipway.

The Port Appin ferry docks at Point;
from the slipway turn right just before the
B8045 onto a faint grassy path that leads
above a pebbly beach. Carry on along the
path as it sweeps right above Lismore's
craggy coastline with views along Loch
Linnhe and over Shuna Island to distant
Beinn a' Bheithir above Ballachulish.
The path curves left around Rubh Aird
Ghainimh to cross a stile at a fence.

From here, a rough path leads beneath
steep craggy slopes on the quieter
western side of Lismore, whose name
derives from the Gaelic *lios-mọr*, meaning
'the Great Garden'. Lismore's fertile
landscape is due to its Dalradian
limestone geology, which supports an
abundance of wildflowers.

Once over a further fence stile, a grassy
path passes a stony bay. Just before
another fence and a craggy outcrop, bear
left uphill through a gap in a wall.
A grassy path now runs southwest across
a field and through another gap in a wall.

74

◄ Port Ramsay Bay

Immediately turn right and continue left of a fence, walking along low cliffs above the shore. There are far-reaching views over Port Ramsay Bay to Mull and, as well as plenty of seabirds on the coastal fringes, there is a chance of seeing golden and white-tailed sea eagles.

As the fence ends, keep straight on across the field and down to a farm track. Turn right and then beyond a gate go left onto a rough road and walk through the settlement of Port Ramsay. A row of whitewashed terraced cottages, each with its own small garden, looks out over Loch Linnhe to Morvern. The village dates back to around 1800 when it provided homes for those working in the lime and fishing industries.

At a telephone box, the road swings left and cuts across the island through peaceful countryside with views eastwards to Beinn Sgulaird above Loch Creran and, further south, Ben Cruachan. After a gate beside a cattle grid, the road veers right and culminates at the B8045. Turn left to head northeast along this minor road, watching out for traffic. There are a few gentle ups and downs as the road extends for 1.5km back to Point and the return journey across the Lynn of Lorn to Port Appin.

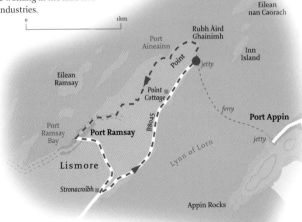

A Salen circular

Distance **9km** Time **2 hours 45**
Terrain **coastal paths, minor roads; hilly**
Map **OS Explorer 376** Access **Oban is well
served by buses and trains; daily ferry
sailings from Oban to Lismore**

Lismore's industrial history centres on
limestone quarrying. Much of it took place
at Salen, on the island's north coast, and
this route passes through what remains of
this small industrial hub. It is a hilly
route, predominantly along quiet roads,
where a stop-off at the Lismore Gaelic
Heritage Centre, with its fascinating
glimpses of the island's history and an
excellent café, may be well timed.

The Oban to Lismore car ferry docks at
the small village of Achnacroish. From the
slipway, walk along the road which passes
a phonebox before winding steeply uphill,

passing Lismore Primary School along
the way. After another 1km of mostly
steady climbing, you meet the B8045.

Turn left here to follow this narrow road
for nearly 500m, then turn right onto a
side road for Frackersaig and Achinduin.
A scenic stretch of the route meanders
across Lismore for another 1km to a rough
track on the right for Salen.

Follow this northeast as it descends
to the remote northern coast of Lismore.
The track runs beneath steep cliffs and
along the shore, fording a burn beside a
limekiln and passing an old cottage ruin.
The silence here is only broken by the
gurgling of the burn and any wildlife that
may be present.

Carry on towards the quay and quarry
to explore the remains of the island's
limestone industry. The stone was

To
Port Ramsay

museum

Lismore

Loch Baile a'
Ghobhainn

0   1km

Grogan
Dubh

Balliveolan

Balnagown

monument

Salen   quarry

B8045

Baligrundle

pier

Achnacroish

Frackersaig

ferry

Kilcheran
Loch

To
Kilcheran

quarried and shipped out on locally-owned smacks (a traditional fishing boat) for agriculture and building mortar between 1826 and the 1930s. Many of the buildings here date from the early days of the quarry, including a manager's office, workers' cottages, a shop and a cottage on the pier. It is an evocative spot, hemmed in on its southern side by the quarry and with some lovely sea views.

At a junction, turn right onto a track that is easily followed as it rises gradually inland. At its high point, there are good views to Mull. Once through a gate and past a couple of houses, carry on to regain the B8045.

Turn left and walk for 1.25km, passing the distinctive Lismore Gaelic Heritage Centre (seasonal opening), to reach a turning on the right for Balnagown. This narrow road takes you southwards, initially rising but soon dropping through picturesque countryside past the peaceful Loch Baile a' Ghobhainn and back to Lismore's south coast and a solitary house at Balnagown.

Go straight on through a gate, now following a path downhill past the remains of an old flax mill to a cottage. Go through a gate to its right and continue to a large cross in memory of Waverley Arthur Cameron, who drowned off the coast here in 1891. The cross was erected by his father Duncan, who, for a period, owned the *Oban Times*, and invented the Waverley pen nib.

After another gate, a coastal path leads to Achnacroish. Here, go through two gates, pass a few cottages onto a track and then, at a junction, turn left to return to the pier.

◀ Limestone workhouses, Salen

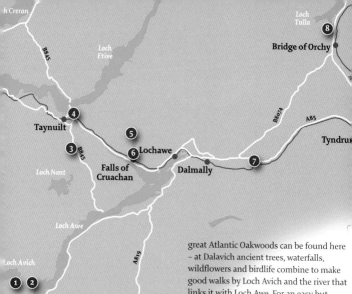

The landscape east of Oban is one of contrasts, from big soaring peaks to waterfalls and serene woodland. As well as its natural beauty, there is plenty to remind you here of the region's industrial heritage. During the 18th and 19th centuries in Glen Nant, a few miles south of Taynuilt, hundreds of people worked in the oakwoods to supply charcoal for the Bonawe Iron Furnace. It is now a peaceful National Nature Reserve in the care of Historic Scotland and is perfect for spotting wildlife.

As at Crinan, remnants of Scotland's great Atlantic Oakwoods can be found here – at Dalavich ancient trees, waterfalls, wildflowers and birdlife combine to make good walks by Loch Avich and the river that links it with Loch Awe. For an easy but entertaining woodland trail, Strone Woods, near Dalmally, is also hard to beat.

To the north of Dalavich rises one of Scotland's finest mountains. Ben Cruachan (often referred to as the 'Hollow Mountain' because of the power station that sits deep within its slopes) will be in the top ten of many hillwalkers' favourite peaks. This is a tough walk and beyond the capabilities of many walkers. An excellent alternative is to climb to Cruachan Dam via the Falls of Cruachan path for an overview of this magnificent landscape.

More sweeping views can be enjoyed from the little hill of Mam Carraigh, which rises above Bridge of Orchy and is approached along a section of Scotland's most famous long-distance walking route, the West Highland Way.

Loch Awe to Bridge of Orchy

The Loch Avich Trail

Distance 8km **Time** 2 hours 30
Terrain woodland, moorland, lochside
and riverside paths **Map** OS Explorer 360
Access buses from Oban to Dalavich

Loch Avich sits at the northern edge of
Inverliever Forest, 2km west of Loch Awe
with the River Avich linking the two
freshwater lochs. This attractive route
passes through some remote countryside
and across a diverse landscape of woods,
moors and waterside, with plenty of
wildlife and views.

Barnaline car park is around 2km north
of Dalavich. Take the path waymarked in
red/yellow for Loch Avich to head
southwards through the ancient Dalavich

Atlantic Oakwood. When you reach a
junction, turn right onto another path to
pass the old Barnaline stable block. The
horses from these stables were used to
transport wood from the forest during
timber operations that took place here in
the mid-20th century. The oak woodland
of Dalavich was also coppiced for charcoal
during the late 1800s.

A grassy path climbs steadily through
mixed woodland where views open out
across Loch Awe. Keep an eye out for red
squirrels. When the path splits, keep right
for Loch Avich, following yellow
waymarks. The trail climbs past a
substantial old stone sheep fank to a
broad forestry track. Go left and walk west

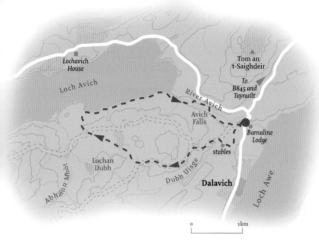

Lochavich
House

Loch Avich

River Avich

Avich
Falls

Tom an
t-Saighdeir

To
B845 and
Taynuilt

Barnaline
Lodge

stables

Lochan
Dubh

Abhainn Mhòr

Dubh Uisge

Dalavich

Loch Awe

0   1km

through conifer woodland to a junction, turning left again here. Follow this to a waymarked path on the right.

This path takes you northwest through woodland and then open countryside. It is a remote and quite lovely little section with good views across the local countryside. After nearly 1.25km, it drops down quite steeply to a crossroads.

Go straight on to accompany a path on its descent through mixed woodland. This marks the start of the finest part of this walk, passing through more ancient oak woodland where finches, blue-, long-tailed-, great- and coal-tits, goldcrest and tree creepers are regular visitors with pied flycatcher and redstart occasionally spotted. The path drops to the banks of Loch Avich where views extend to

Lochavich House and to the higher slopes of Cruach Narrachan.

Continuing east above the banks of the loch and lined with native oaks, the trail is delightfully peaceful. Eventually, it swings right as the loch drains into the River Avich to now follow the river's southern bank through mixed woodland.

When you come to a wide forestry track, turn left and cross a bridge over the water, then immediately go right onto a track that runs above the River Avich's northern bank. After 300m, a blue waymarked path on your right leads you down to a footbridge that crosses back over the river, with a short, steep climb on the other side taking you up above its banks. Continue until the path concludes at a wide track, turning left here to reach the start.

Avich Falls

Distance 3km Time 1 hour
Terrain riverside paths with some ups and
downs Map OS Explorer 360
Access buses from Oban to Dalavich

A short waymarked loop meanders easily
along the banks of the River Avich and
through a section of the renowned
Dalavich Oakwood, passing the
spectacular Avich Falls along the way.

Barnaline car park is around 2km north
of Dalavich. Take the wide forestry track
marked with blue waymarks as it winds
gradually uphill. After around 200m, turn
right onto a path signposted for the
Avich Falls. This enters an enchanting
broadleaf woodland with views down

into the clear waters of the River Avich,
where several waterfalls help the river
make its way towards Loch Awe.

The path swings right and then left,
dropping down to the riverbank and
continuing through the predominantly
oak woodland, once part of the great
Atlantic Oakwoods that extended across
much of Europe's Atlantic coast from
Spain to Scotland.

The damp, humid climate with high
rainfall and acidic soils provided the
perfect conditions to create this temperate
rainforest. The woodland here is now a
Site of Special Scientific Interest (SSSI)
where fungi, mosses, liverworts lichen and
many species of ferns thrive along with a

selection of wildflowers in spring and summer, including bluebells, foxglove and primrose.

The path travels past the lowest section of the Avich Falls and then climbs back up above the river, passing a weir. After another short, steady ascent, it drops down to cross a footbridge over a waterfall and a beautiful pool – look out for dipper and kingfisher along these banks. Once on the other side, continue in the same direction, with the river now to your left, to reach a broad forestry track.

Turn right to follow the track downhill, soon reaching a path on the right that

detours down to the dramatic Avich Falls – three natural tiers with the torrent of whitewater spanning the width of the river make for an impressive natural spectacle, particularly after heavy rain.

Return to the main track and carry on downstream above the river, eventually reaching a junction just beyond a gate. Go right onto a narrow road which drops downhill to reach the Kilchrenan/Dalavich road. Turn right to take this road down past several cottages, crossing back over the River Avich at a roadbridge and continuing until you reach Barnaline car park on your right.

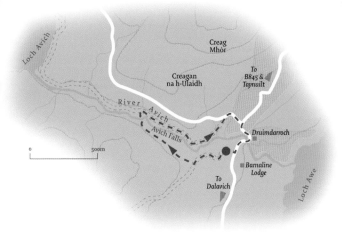

Glen Nant Oakwoods

Distance 4km **Time** 1 hour 30
Terrain woodland paths with several
steep ascents **Map** OS Explorer 377
Access buses from Oban to Glen Nant

It's hard to imagine today, but Glen Nant
was once a busy industrial site with
hundreds of people working in the forest.
For nearly 150 years, trees were coppiced
and charcoal burnt and then transported
to the Bonawe Iron Furnace. Glen Nant
has been a Site of Special Scientific
Interest since 1961 and is now a National
Nature Reserve. Its oakwoods are home to
many wildflowers, including a spectacular
covering of bluebells in spring.

Glen Nant National Nature Reserve lies
5km south of Taynuilt on the west side of
the B845. Look out for the signed forestry
track which leads to a small car park. Glen
Nant means 'Glen of the Nettles' and has
links to a medieval Christian site; the
wood's historic name is *Coille Braigh na*

Cille, 'The Wood of the Brae of the Church'.

Follow the forestry track uphill through
a gate into woodland with the River Nant
below to the right. After around 500m, the
track swings left to reach a waymark
pointing right. Take this path for an
ascent which is at first gradual and then
steepens through oakwoods to emerge
high above the glen with views opening
out to Ben Cruachan.

Bluebells, wood sorrel, primrose, wood
anemone and ramsons carpet the
woodland floor in spring and you may spot
red squirrels. There are also several large
anthills, constructed by wood ants, which
play a vital role in the ecosystem here.

After dropping steadily, the path
undulates gently and winds through the
trees. Another fairly steep dip takes you
down to a bridge over a burn.

Roughly east of here the River Nant
narrows at a point known as Tailor's Leap,
so called because of an enterprising local

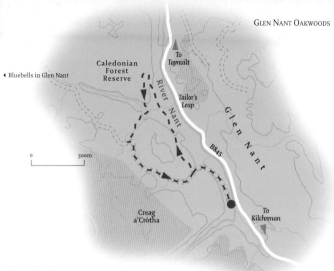

◀ Bluebells in Glen Nant

tailor said to have operated an illicit whisky, using these narrows to flee the excise men. Also associated with the tailor is the settlement of Larach a' Chrotail, or 'Lichen House', where people brought cloth to be dyed with lichen: the ruins lie near the walk start point.

Shortly after crossing the burn, the path forks. Keep right for a steady climb to a bench with a view that extends to the mountains of Glen Etive.

The oak trees of Glen Nant were coppiced and then burned for charcoal from the 1750s, when Bonawe Iron Furnace opened. At the industry's height, more than 600 people worked here with the charcoal transported by pack ponies along tracks to Bonawe.

As well as charcoal, the bark from oak trees was crucial to the leather tanning industry. After Bonawe Iron Furnace

closed in 1876, coppicing of the Glen Nant oaks ceased and the wood has since returned to its natural state.

After another ascent, the path turns left to cross a section of boardwalk, before dropping down a series of zigzags and then steps. The path veers left to run above the Eas Achadh Airigh (a tributary of the River Nant) which you soon cross by a bridge.

Continue to climb steadily through the wood and, at a junction, turn left. A path carries on in a southwest direction, crossing a footbridge over the Eas na Caorach Duibhe with another steady ascent to gain a forestry track. Turn left here. With woodland to the north and open views to the south, this leads past the point where you took the waymarked path on the outward route and all the way back down to the car park.

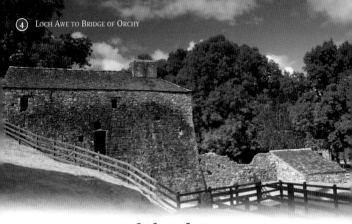

To Bonawe and the shore

Distance 5km **Time** 1 hour 30
Terrain woodland and countryside paths
and tracks, minor road **Map** OS Explorer
377 **Access** no public transport to the start

During the 18th and 19th centuries,
several of Argyll's oakwoods provided
charcoal for the Bonawe Iron Furnace that
stood near the southern bank of Loch
Etive a little north of Taynuilt. Today the
furnace is cared for by Historic Scotland
and provides a focal point for this
straightforward but fascinating walk.

The walk begins from Inverawe
Smokehouse, 2.5km northwest of Bridge
of Awe. Just before the shop and visitor
centre, turn right and walk down a path,
which bears left before a pond. Go
through a gate into a field to follow a
faint path to a distinctive suspension
bridge that spans the River Awe, a popular
spot with anglers.

Once across, carry straight on across
another field and, at its right corner,
go through a gate and turn right onto
a track. This heads northwest
through woodland, with views of
the surrounding countryside.

In a while, it veers left to run alongside
a stretch of beech woodland and then
past Bonawe Lodge House. Bonawe
House, once the home of the iron furnace
manager, stands behind.

Exit the woodland beside a few cottages
at Brochroy. Turn right down a road, cross
the access road for Bonawe House, then
go through a gate and follow a track that
drops downhill to Bonawe Iron Furnace.
The works opened in 1753, mainly due to
the abundance of oakwoods nearby
– the oak was burned for charcoal that
fired the furnace.

At its height Bonawe Iron Furnace
produced 700 tons of pig iron ore every
year, employing around 20 people at the
furnace and a further 600 locals producing

◀ Bonawe Iron Furnace Wheel Pit

charcoal in the woods. Pig iron was the mainstay of the furnace but it also made cannonballs during the Napoleonic Wars of the early 19th century.

The furnace closed in 1876 but many of the buildings have been restored, providing a good impression of how it would have looked when in operation. Bonawe Iron Furnace is open daily from April to September (there is an admission charge).

Continue to reach the B845. Turn right onto this, then left to reach Airds Bay and an old jetty, Kelly's Pier, that juts out into Loch Etive. Walk along the stony beach,

breathing in the salty air of this seawater loch. After a whitewashed cottage, a grassy path veers right back to the B845. Turn left to reach another jetty.

The loch draws the eye northeast to the mighty slopes of Ben Starav on the near shore, while rising to your right is Stob Dearg, the westernmost top of Ben Cruachan, better known as the Taynuilt Peak. This is a tranquil spot where you may spy otters on the water's edge and golden or white-tailed sea eagles high on the thermals above.

Return to the Bonawe Furnace access road, then retrace your steps to Inverawe.

Ben Cruachan

Distance 11km **Time** 6 hours
Terrain woodland and mountain paths,
several steep ascents and some bouldery
ground; the descent over Meall Cuanail is
pathless **Map** OS Explorer 377
Access trains from Glasgow and Oban to
Falls of Cruachan; buses to Cruachan
Power Station

Ben Cruachan is one of the most popular
of all of Scotland's high mountains, and
with good reason. A tough route on mostly
good paths, it is a beautiful peak with
iconic views. For a circular route, it is worth
combining this with a climb over Meall
Cuanail, though the descent is on pathless
ground and best left for a clear day.

The walk begins from the A85 just east
of the excellent Cruachan Dam Visitor
Centre. The car park is only for those
making use of the centre.

Climb the steps (signposted for the

Falls of Cruachan) towards Falls of
Cruachan Railway Station. Just before the
platform, pass under the railway line and
continue to a path on the left. A steep
ascent proceeds through woodland high
above the eastern side of the Allt
Cruachan gorge.

After climbing a tall stile over a deer
fence, the path continues across open
hillside to gain the Cruachan Dam access
road and a view of Ben Cruachan's pointed
peak. Turn left, cross a bridge over the
river and, once beneath the enormous
dam wall, turn left over a low fence. An
indistinct path rises to meet a track, which
is followed along the western side of the
reservoir, looking to Coire Cruachan.

After 1.25km, at the reservoir's northern
tip, the track ends. Turn left onto an
initially faint path that runs to the right of
a fast-flowing burn. The path improves as
it climbs steadily west into Coire Dearg, a

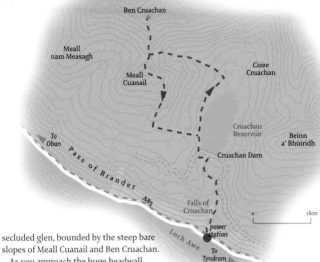

secluded glen, bounded by the steep bare slopes of Meall Cuanail and Ben Cruachan.

As you approach the huge headwall, the gradient steepens to gain Bealach an Lochain at a height of 840m. There is a tiny loch that gives the pass its name and, in clear weather, the views of Mull are wonderful.

Turn right for the climb north with large boulders to cross. The path can be vague and care is required to reach Ben Cruachan's compact 1126m summit and an outlook of immense proportions. To the northeast, the eye is led along Loch Etive to the Glen Etive and Glen Coe mountains while, on a good day, the Isle of Rum's spiky outline is visible to the northwest.

Carefully descend back to the bealach, paying attention to the steep, awkward ground. From here, you can retrace your steps, but to make this a circular

expedition climb south alongside old fenceposts to reach Meall Cuanail's 918m top and a stunning view of Ben Cruachan's flowing ridge. Ben Cruachan means 'Heap on the Mountain', referring to the conical peak that towers above the ridge.

The initial part of the descent keeps left of the fenceposts, dropping east and then south over pathless ground. Once you reach a flatter, boggier section, the fence veers away southwest. From here, pick a line in an easterly direction – the grassy ground is relatively easy to cover, only steepening when it drops down to regain the track near the Cruachan Dam wall. Take the outward route back to Loch Awe.

◄ Loch Etive from Ben Cruachan

Falls of Cruachan and the Dam

Distance 4km **Time** 1 hour 30
Terrain steep woodland paths, minor
road **Map** OS Explorer 377 **Access** trains
from Glasgow and Oban to Falls of
Cruachan; buses to Cruachan
Power Station

Ben Cruachan is beyond the physical
limits of many walkers, but an excellent
alternative is the well-made woodland
path that climbs steeply above the Falls
of Cruachan to reach Cruachan Dam.
Here, the grandeur of the landscape can
be appreciated without the rigours of Ben
Cruachan's unforgiving slopes.

The walk begins from the A85 just east
of Cruachan Visitor Centre, home to a café
and an exhibition detailing the history of
'The Hollow Mountain'; there are also
guided tours into the mountain (open
daily in summer and Monday to Friday in
winter). The car park is only for those
making use of the centre.

Climb the steps (signposted for the
Falls of Cruachan) towards Falls of
Cruachan Railway Station. Just before the
platform, pass under the railway line and
continue to a path on the left. From here,
begin to climb through birch and oak
woodland. Once over a little burn, the
path now zigzags as it ascends a little
more steeply above the east side of the
Allt Cruachan gorge – the tumbling Falls
of Cruachan can be heard below.

The steep climb persists above the
treeline where you are rewarded with a
view of the long arm of Loch Awe as it
stretches southwest towards the

◀ Loch Awe

Coire
Cruachan

Cruachan
Reservoir

Cruachan Dam

Beinn a' Bhuiridh

To
Oban

Pass of Brander

A85

Falls of
Cruachan

power
station

To
Tyndrum

Loch Awe

0   1km

Argyll Coast. Below you is the Pass of Brander where Robert the Bruce defeated Clan MacDougall in 1309.

After rising more steadily up the wooded hillside, the route brings you to a deer fence. Crossing this by a high stile, the path now heads over open hillside. Above, Ben Cruachan's long high ridge presents a formidable barrier while the Allt Cruachan rushes downhill through a sequence of attractive rocky pools.

As you approach the access road, things can get a little boggy underfoot. Turn right onto the access road and then left to climbs steeply under Beinn a' Bhuiridh. Where the road splits, bear right and continue through a gate onto the dam wall for views along the reservoir into Coire Cruachan and southeast to the Crianlarich mountains and the Arrochar Alps.

Construction of this engineering feat began in the early 1960s and it opened in 1965 – but not before 1500 workers had been employed here and 220,000 cubic metres of rock and soil had been excavated from the mountain slopes below Ben Cruachan. The cavern is the size of a football pitch and access to the turbines is through a 1km-long tunnel.

Four generators are capable of generating 440 megawatts of electricity, enough to supply more than 225,000 homes.

Make your way across the top of the 316m-long dam and at its far end pass through a gate, turn left onto a track, then, just after a small car park, go left again. Walk down an indistinct path to a fence directly beneath the dam. This is easily crossed onto a road. Turn right and follow this downhill to meet the outward path, where you go right again and retrace your steps down to Loch Awe.

Strone Woods stroll

**Distance 2.25km Time 45 minutes
Terrain woodland paths Map OS Explorer
377 Access buses from Glasgow and Oban
to Strone Woods access road end**

This simple, short walk follows good
paths around the attractive Strone Woods
and is suitable for all ages. For the most
part, the route follows the dramatic
surge of the River Lochy as it carves
its way through the western fringe
of Glen Lochy.

Begin from the small car park,
signposted as Strone Hill, which sits on
the south side of the A85, just over 5km
east of Dalmally. Bounded by big peaks
such as Ben Lui and Beinn Udlaidh, Glen
Lochy may mean 'Glen of the Black
Goddess' or 'Glen of the Black River',

referring to the River Lochy. Drovers used
to rest their cattle here as they headed
south to the markets of southern
Scotland and northern England.

Pass between the two stone seats and
take a clear well-made path on the left.
This rises gradually into oak woodland,
initially following red waymarks, with
good views of the surrounding hills,
particularly Beinn na Sroine. Soon veering
right, it descends gradually before
meandering through the woodland,
where rowan and birch complement the
lichen-covered oaks.

The path then runs above the steep
gorge of the River Lochy with its rushing
waters plunging through the landscape.
At a junction, it is worth going left for a
short detour downhill where you can

◀ Strone Woods

enjoy views of a dramatic waterfall.

Return to the main path and walk left, with views of the giants of Beinn Eunaich and Beinn a'Chochuill above Glen Strae. At a green waymarked junction, go left and when the path splits take the right branch to carry on through the woodland, listening out for woodpecker, wood warbler and pied flycatcher.

After crossing a footbridge over a burn, the path continues high above the gorge with the sound of the tumbling waters below. At the next fork, keep left and in due course the path sweeps right away from the river to rise gradually alongside pine woodland. A gentle descent then returns to the outward path.

Turn left and follow this to the next junction, going left here to arrive back at the car park.

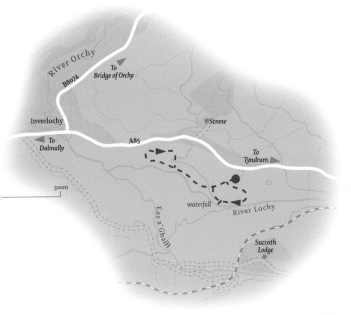

Mam Carraigh by the Way

Distance **9km** Time **2 hours 30**
Terrain **hillside paths, minor road**
Map **OS Explorer 377 Access trains from Glasgow and Mallaig to Bridge of Orchy. Buses from Glasgow and Fort William to Bridge of Orchy**

Bridge of Orchy is the start point for this walk that follows part of the West Highland Way to climb to the vantage point of Mam Carraigh. Inveroran and its historic 18th-century coaching inn is the next port of call before the return on a quiet road which runs alongside Loch Tulla and the River Orchy.

Bridge of Orchy translates from Gaelic as 'Bridge of the Woody Stream Place'. The River Orchy runs beneath the 18th-century stone bridge that was built as part of General Wade's and Major Caulfeild's military road scheme. The Munro peaks of Beinn Dorain and Beinn an Dothaidh frame a small collection of houses and a hotel.

From the railway station, walk down to the A82, cross over onto the old military road and follow this over the Bridge of Orchy. As the road swings right, march on ahead onto the West Highland Way (you are still on the route of the old military road). The West Highland Way extends for 154km from Milngavie on the outskirts of Glasgow to Fort William.

A path climbs through a gate and then continues along the edge of woodland, with views opening out across Bridge of

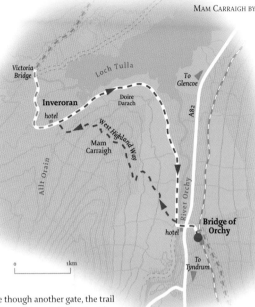

Orchy. Once though another gate, the trail enters conifer woods and climbs steadily northwest, soon exiting onto open hillside and then curving left.

As the path rises gradually above the treeline, it's worth pausing to look back at Beinn Odhar and Beinn a' Chaisteil above Tyndrum, as well as the steep sides of Beinn Achaladair to the northeast.

More views await at the top of Mam Carraigh, with the West Highland Way tapering around the flanks of the Black Mount to the north, while to the northwest the Abhainn Shira drains from lonely Loch Dochard into Loch Tulla. Below is the Inveroran Hotel.

The stony West Highland Way drops northwest and then west down to a minor road, with the Inveroran to the left. This has been a popular watering hole and staging post since it opened in 1707, with such luminaries as Samuel Coleridge, Dorothy Wordsworth and Charles Dickens all having visited here.

Turn right at the road to leave the West Highland Way behind, following the road between the shores of Loch Tulla and the picturesque stands of Scots pine that cover the slopes of Doire Darach.

In a little under 2km, the road curves right to bring you ever closer to the banks of the River Orchy in the shadow of first Beinn an Dothaidh and then Beinn Dorain as it returns you to Bridge of Orchy.

Index